CONVERSATIONS
WITH SCRIPTURE:

THE ACTS OF
THE APOSTLES

Other Books in the Series

CONVERSATIONS
WITH SCRIPTURE:

THE ACTS OF
THE APOSTLES

C. K. ROBERTSON

MP Morehouse Publishing
NEW YORK · HARRISBURG · DENVER

Morehouse Publishing, 4775 Linglestown Road, Harrisburg, PA 17112

Morehouse Publishing, 445 Fifth Avenue, New York, NY 10016

Morehouse Publishing is an imprint of Church Publishing Incorporated.

www.churchpublishing.org

Cover art: Icon of the Descent of the Holy Spirit on Pentecost, Distributed by Trisagion Arts, Valparaiso, Indiana

Icon written at the facilities of "Orant" Religious Art, Lviv, Ukraine

Series cover design by Corey Kent

Series design by Beth Oberholtzer

Library of Congress Cataloging-in-Publication Data

Robertson, C. K. (Charles Kevin), 1964–
    Conversations with Scripture : the Acts of the Apostles / C.K. Robertson.
      p.   cm.
    Includes bibliographical references (p.   ) and index.
    ISBN 978-0-8192-2372-2 (pbk. : alk. paper)
    ISBN 978-0-8192-2724-9 (Ebook)
    ISBN 978-0-8192-2737-9 (Kindle)
    1. Bible. N.T. Acts—Criticism, interpretation, etc. I. Title.
BS2625.52.R63   2010
226.6'06—dc22

2010012898

Printed in the United States of America

10 11 12 13 14 15   10 9 8 7 6 5 4 3 2 1

For Floyd and Berry Trogdon,
Gifts of God in my life and ministry

O God of unchangeable power and eternal light: Let the whole world see and know that things which were being cast down are being raised up, and things which had grown old are being made new, and that all things are being brought to their perfection by him through whom all things were made, your Son Jesus Christ our Lord.

AMEN.

CONTENTS

INTRODUCTION
TO THE SERIES

ANGLICAN ASSOCIATION OF BIBLICAL SCHOLARS STUDY SERIES

To talk about a distinctively Anglican approach to Scripture is a daunting task. Within any one part of the larger church that we call the Anglican Communion there is, on historical grounds alone, an enormous variety. But as the global character of the church becomes apparent in ever-newer ways, the task of accounting for that variety while naming the characteristics of a distinctive approach becomes increasingly difficult.

In addition, the examination of Scripture is not confined to formal studies of the kind addressed in this series of parish studies written by formally trained biblical scholars. Systematic theologian David Ford, who participated in the Lambeth Conference of 1998, rightly noted that although "most of us have studied the Bible over many years" and "are aware of various academic approaches to it," we have "also lived in it" and "inhabited it, through worship, preaching, teaching and meditation." As such, Ford observes, "The Bible in the Church is like a city we have lived in for a long time." We may not be able to account for the history of every building or the architecture on every street, but we know our way around and it is a source of life to each of us.[1]

That said, we have not done as much as we should in acquainting the inhabitants of that famed city with the architecture that lies within. So, as risky as it may seem, it is important to set out an introduction to the highlights of that city—which this series proposes to

---

1. David F. Ford, "The Bible, the World and the Church I," in *The Official Report of the Lambeth Conference 1998*, ed. J. Mark Dyer et al. (Harrisburg, PA: Morehouse Publishing, 1999), 332.

explore at length. Perhaps the best way in which to broach that task is to provide a handful of descriptors.

The first of those descriptors that leaps to mind is familiar, basic, and forever debated: *authoritative*. Years ago I was asked by a colleague who belonged to the Evangelical Free Church why someone with as much obvious interest in the Bible would be an Episcopal priest. I responded, "Because we read the whole of Scripture and not just the parts of it that suit us." Scripture has been and continues to play a singular role in the life of the Anglican Communion, but it has rarely been used in the sharply prescriptive fashion that has characterized some traditions.

Some have characterized this approach as an attempt to navigate a *via media* between overbearing control and an absence of accountability. But I think it is far more helpful to describe the tensions not as a matter of steering a course between two different and competing priorities, but as the complex dance necessary to live under a very different, but typically Anglican notion of authority itself. Authority shares the same root as the word "to author" and as such, refers first and foremost, not to the *power* to *control* with all that both of those words suggest, but to the capacity to *author creativity*, with all that both of those words suggest.[2] As such, the function of Scripture is to carve out a creative space in which the work of the Holy Spirit can yield the very kind of fruit associated with its work in the church. The difficulty, of course, is that for that space to be creative, it is also necessary for it to have boundaries, much like the boundaries we establish for other kinds of genuinely creative freedom—the practice of scales for concert pianists, the discipline of work at the barre that frees the ballerina, or the guidance that parents provide for their children. Defined in this way, it is possible to see the boundaries around that creative space as barriers to be eliminated, or as walls that provide protection, but they are neither.

And so the struggle continues with the authority of Scripture. From time to time in the Anglican Communion, it has been and will

---

2. For my broader understanding of authority, I am indebted to Eugene Kennedy and Sara C. Charles, *Authority: The Most Misunderstood Idea in America* (New York: Free Press, 1997).

be treated as a wall that protects us from the complexity of navigating without error the world in which we live. At other times, it will be treated as the ancient remains of a city to be cleared away in favor of a brave new world. But both approaches are rooted, not in the limitations of Scripture, but in our failure to welcome the creative space we have been given.

For that reason, at their best, Anglican approaches to Scripture are also *illuminative*. William Sloane Coffin once observed that the problem with Americans and the Bible is that we read it like a drunk uses a lamppost. We lean on it, we don't use it for illumination.[3] Leaning on Scripture—or having the lamppost taken out completely—are simply two very closely related ways of failing to acknowledge the creative space provided by Scripture. But once the creative space is recognized for what it is, then the importance of reading Scripture illuminatively becomes apparent. Application of the insight Scripture provides into who we are and what we might become is not something that can be prescribed or mapped out in detail. It is only a conversation with Scripture, marked by humility, that can begin to spell out the particulars. Reading Scripture is, then, in the Anglican tradition a delicate and demanding task, that involves both the careful listening for the voice of God and courageous conversation with the world around us.

It is, for that reason, an approach that is also marked by *critical engagement* with the text itself. It is no accident that from 1860 to 1900 the three best-known names in the world of biblical scholarship were Anglican priests, the first two of whom were bishops: B. F. Westcott, J. B. Lightfoot, and F. J. A. Hort. Together the three made contributions to both the church and the critical study of the biblical text that became a defining characteristic of Anglican life.

Of the three, Westcott's contribution perhaps best captures the balance. Not only did his work contribute to a critical text of the Greek New Testament that would eventually serve as the basis for the English Revised Version, but as Bishop of Durham he also convened a conference of Christians to discuss the arms race in Europe,

---

3. William Sloane Coffin, *Credo* (Louisville, KY: Westminster John Knox Press, 2003), 156.

founded the Christian Social Union, and mediated the Durham coal strike of 1892.

The English roots of the tradition are not the only, or even the defining characteristic of Anglican approaches to Scripture. The church, no less than the rest of the world, has been forever changed by the process of globalization, which has yielded a rich *diversity* that complements the traditions once identified with the church.

Scripture in Uganda, for example, has been read with an emphasis on private, allegorical, and revivalist applications. The result has been a tradition in large parts of East Africa that stresses the reading of Scripture on one's own; the direct application made to the contemporary situation without reference to the setting of the original text; and the combination of personal testimony with the power of public exhortation.

At the same time, however, globalization has brought that tradition into conversation with people from other parts of the Anglican Communion as the church in Uganda has sought to bring the biblical text to bear on its efforts to address the issues of justice, poverty, war, disease, food shortage, and education. In such a dynamic environment, the only thing that one can say with certainty is that neither the Anglican Communion, nor the churches of East Africa, will ever be the same again.

Authoritative, illuminative, critical, and varied—these are not the labels that one uses to carve out an approach to Scripture that can be predicted with any kind of certainty. Indeed, if the word *dynamic*—just used—is added to the list, perhaps all that one can predict is still more change! And, for that reason, there will be observers who (not without reason) will argue that the single common denominator in this series is that each of the authors also happens to be an Anglican. (There might even be a few who will dispute that!)

But such is the nature of life in any city, including one shaped by the Bible. We influence the shape of its life, but we are also shaped and nurtured by it. And if that city is of God's making, then to force our own design on the streets and buildings around us is to disregard the design that the chief architect has in mind.

—Frederick W. Schmidt
Series Editor

AUTOBIOGRAPHICAL
NOTE

Text and context. From the moment I bought my first Bible at age fifteen, I have been blessed to have mentors who impressed upon me the importance of understanding the scriptural text not as a disembodied entity in some kind of spiritual vacuum, but in terms of a larger context. This context, at once historical, cultural, and canonical, is the world in which any given passage resides, and it is impossible (or, at least, very unwise) to examine that passage outside of all that surrounds it.

Years later, when I pursued my Ph.D. studies on conflict management in 1 Corinthians, I found myself exploring what the first-century world of Paul actually looked like, sounded like, felt like. This led me to Acts. Not that Acts provides a perfectly simple template into which we can place Paul's letters, for indeed there are several instances of complex and difficult issues of reconciliation between the documents. Rather, I went to Acts in much the same way as I would look at Luke's gospel while studying Matthew's; both gospels emerge from their respective contexts and help me see different approaches to a similar event or teaching. And where they differ in details, it is appropriate to ask what Luke means by a particular angle, or what Matthew is saying within his larger argument. Even so, in comprehending the early spread of the good news, it is helpful to see Paul's own letters, but also what Acts has to say, always while being aware of first-century social, political, and religious life.

What happened along the way for me was that, while I began my studies and initial writings with Paul's letters, it was Luke's marvelous story of the development of the early church that soon grabbed my attention. And in reading Acts alongside Luke's gospel, I found myself engaged in a rich and deeply theological story of God's radical, incarnational love for humanity. The texts of passages from Paul's letters became richer, deeper, because of my reading of Acts. And Acts itself challenged me to go further with my studies of that time and its context. What a delight to go, as C. S. Lewis once said, "further up and further in" through Acts.

 # Apostolic Call

*Raise up in this and every land evangelists
and heralds of your kingdom, that your
Church may proclaim the unsearchable
riches of our Savior.*

COLLECT OF A MISSIONARY,
THE BOOK OF COMMON PRAYER

Although it is an anonymous work, from the second century on the general assumption has been that the book of Acts was written by Luke, Paul's sometime traveling companion affectionately described as the "beloved physician" (Col. 4:14). It is noteworthy that the author does not appear overly concerned about being personally acknowledged. Even in those passages where the third-person narrative of the book suddenly shifts to a first-person account, as if the narrator is including himself in the story, the author's identity remains unknown, an unnamed member of Paul's supporting cast. There have been a few scholars in recent years who have questioned Luke's authorship of Acts, but since there has been no conclusive evidence to prove otherwise, we will here follow the ancient and much-accepted tradition and refer to the author as Luke. One thing is clear: Luke certainly knew how to offer his readers an exciting account.

The first and primary recipient of Acts was a character known only as Theophilus (1:1). The Greek name may be translated as "loved by God," "dear to God" or "friend of

1

God." Whoever this Theophilus was, he appears to have been of high social standing, given Luke's earlier designation, "most excellent Theophilus" (Luke 1:3). He may have been Luke's patron or backer, helping fund the writing and distribution of his works. Certainly, Luke displays deference towards Theophilus, yet at the same time gives us a sense that this patron is also a pupil, a catechist who needs to "know the truth concerning the things about which you have been instructed" (Luke 1:4).

Even so, it is clear that Acts, like Luke's gospel, was intended for a wider audience. Indeed, as one New Testament scholar has noted, "Whoever Theophilus was, he is all of us." We are all beloved of God, dear to God. And we, like Theophilus and those other earliest readers, are all recipients of God's good news . . . a generation removed. For neither those first readers nor we can boast having seen and heard Jesus in the flesh, and many then, like now, never encountered the Twelve and other early church leaders in person. Thus, for Theophilus and Luke's other initial readers, Acts fills in the blanks about God's work following Jesus' life, death, and resurrection.

Luke's Sequel: Story or History?

Often referred to as Luke's "sequel," Acts has long been understood as the second in a two-volume work, in which the gospel account focuses on the life and work of Jesus from before his birth to his death and resurrection, and Acts picks up the story from that point and gives attention to the exploits of the inheritors of Jesus' mission and ministry.

At the same time, it should be noted that those church leaders who put together the canon of the New Testament placed Acts not directly after Luke, but rather after Matthew, Mark, Luke, and John together. All four gospels were included together, forming a multi-faceted genre, each piece balancing the nuances and emphases of the others. It is noteworthy, moreover, that Acts was chosen to follow all four together, thereby serving as a sequel not only to Luke but also to the entire gospel tradition.

Acts thus serves as an ideal bridge between the four gospels and the various epistles, revealing a crucial part of the Christian story. Without it, we might well wonder how a small, Palestinian-based,

Jewish sectarian movement became the geographically expansive and ethnically diverse phenomenon that we encounter in Paul's letters. For that matter, Acts helps us understand how Paul, a character who does not even appear in the gospel accounts, suddenly is center-stage in the history of the Christian church. Truly, it is a bridge document.

It would be difficult, however, to describe Acts as "history" in the modern sense. It certainly does not fit into the seemingly neat category of objective reporting of facts with its descriptions of miracles, visions, and divine guidance. Of course, it is important for us to note that objective reporting as we define it today is something of an illusion. It has often been said that "history is written by the winners," and there is some truth to this. Ironically, today the field has broadened considerably, so that histories are being written from many views and vantage points. Revisionist histories are flourishing, as is the genre of literature known as "historical fiction." In an age of 24/7 news coverage, it is becoming accepted that even the best histories are in some way subjective, even if only in terms of what is included and what is left out.

It is clear at the start of Acts that Luke's goal is to follow up on the "orderly account" (Lk. 1:1) of his gospel, which told "all the Jesus did and taught from the beginning" (Acts 1:1), picking up at the point where the other left off. Unlike his "former treatise," however, Acts would not have three other narratives against which to check its reporting; in the New Testament, the only balancing agent to Luke's reporting of the church's early days is the collection of Paul's letters. Comparisons between Paul's and Luke's reminiscences of the same or similar events (such as the Jerusalem Council or the relationship between Paul and Peter) reveal the kind of nuanced differences that comparisons between the gospels also show about what really happened. If we want to read Acts as a kind of ancient historical account, it is important to read Paul's take on things as well. It is not that one is right and the other wrong—again, such distinctions arise from a false assumption of "objective" history—but that Luke viewed Paul and Peter and the rest of those leaders in ways that Paul himself did not. As we include Acts and the epistles together, then we begin to understand better that crucial period in the church's history.

Acts is, of course, more than history. It is also story, a very lively story—Luke's success story of early Christianity. This is obvious from the start, as Jesus predicts the ever-expanding geographical parameters that will result from the work of his "witnesses" (1:8). Almost immediately after Jesus' departure from the scene, we see impressive—no, explosive—growth on the day of Pentecost. The increasing numbers and deepening commitment that Luke details are key markers still used by parishes and dioceses today to denote success, but it is the way Luke tells the tale of such growth that makes Acts come alive. Those opening geographical parameters ("beginning at Jerusalem, through Judea and Samaria, to the ends of the earth") provide the direction for the movement, which Luke then couples with a momentous energy that propels the story forward in a way that most novelists would envy. Action, suspense, drama: Acts has it all, not to mention magicians, shipwrecks and, in Acts 5, a literally drop-dead approach to Christian stewardship. If Paul's letters address all the dysfunctions of later Christian communities, Luke's saga instead shows the next generation what they could aspire to be. Acts is truly a story that is hard to put down.

The Lobbyist and the Theologian

Readers throughout the years have noticed Luke's apparent desire to build a bridge between the young Christian movement and the Roman Empire in which it was born. Luke not only paints Roman officials in a positive light, especially in Paul's ongoing trial in the later chapters of the book, but also shows that Christianity was in no way considered a threat to Roman interests. In his earlier gospel, he offered significant moments of recognition on the part of Romans such as the centurion at the foot of the cross who declared at Jesus' death, "Certainly this man was innocent [or righteous]" (Luke 23:47), a different statement than that attributed to the soldier in Mark and Matthew ("Truly this man was God's Son!"-Mk. 15:39; Mt. 27:54). Although it is not Luke's primary theme, the author continuously shows in Acts how the growing Jesus movement was "innocent," a *religio licita* or "acceptable religion" in the empire, and one intimately connected with its Jewish "parent." Indeed, in Acts 18:12–17, the Roman official Gallio rules that any conflicts between this

Christian movement and its Jewish neighbors is an internal affair, since Christianity was born out of Judaism. There is, admittedly, consistent opposition to the new faith from Jewish leaders throughout Acts, hinting at the rivalry between church and synagogue in Luke's own time following the destruction of the Jerusalem temple. Yet Luke will go out of his way to tie Christianity firmly in with Judaism, showing through ongoing references to and from the Hebrew Scriptures how the new faith fulfilled, not abrogated, the promises of God to Israel, even as it opened the gates of salvation to non-Jews. In this way Acts makes a strong political case for the acceptance of Christianity by both Jews and Romans.

However, the book is also an extended theological argument for the work of God in and through our spiritual ancestors, fragile and fallible like us. Yes, as in other parts of Scripture God is the chief Actor in the play, unseen but always behind the events that reveal themselves. And, yes, there are moments in Acts when otherworldly angelic beings suddenly appear, heralds of divine message. But most of the time the focus is on flesh and blood heralds and heroes, the fragile, fallible, altogether human people who carry the message and mission of Jesus forward. Acts is an utterly incarnational book. It has miracles, signs of power that point to the inescapable power of God bursting into our world, but the most profound miracle in Acts might well be the growth of the church itself, usually against the odds and in spite of opposition both within and without. Any smart film director today will tell you that it does not matter how impressive the special effects are if you do not have a solid story and strong characters. One might well argue that Luke has both.

If a movie were made of Acts, some of the key casting choices predictably would be for recognizable figures such as Peter, James, and John. The title of the book is, after all, the Acts of the Apostles, and the stage has already been set in the first half of Luke's two-part series for these leaders to rise to prominence. It is, therefore, all the more surprising that it is not the names of Peter and the rest of the Twelve that appear again and again as the story progresses, but rather unexpected and previously unknown figures like Barnabas, Stephen, Philip, Timothy, Priscilla and Aquila, and Paul of Tarsus. The plot twist here is that the "stars," the designated apostles, disappear altogether by the time the tale has barely reached its midpoint, while these other apostolic workers become the true protagonists. Even Luke himself seizes some time on the boards, as his use of the third person plural, "they," shifts in the latter part of the story to the first person plural "we," as he describes the shipwreck of Paul and his followers on the island of Malta and includes himself among them (28:1ff). And as in some avant-garde production, by the time the curtain falls that "we" even includes us, as Luke's open-ended finale suggests that the apostolic commission pronounced by Jesus all the way back in chapter one will only really be fulfilled when we, the audience, become co-participants in the mission.

One final thing that should be noted about the theological dimension of Acts is the prominent place given to the speeches and sermons, which together comprise almost one-third of the book. Whether it is Peter, Paul, or Stephen speaking, the various monologues offer strong summaries of the essential points of faith for those earliest Christians, always focused on Jesus and the salvation that comes through his death and resurrection. Repetition is also used to strengthen readers' awareness of certain key points or events; for example, the story of Peter's encounter with Cornelius and Paul's conversion on the Damascus Road are both repeated three times.

The End is the Beginning

Matthew's gospel concludes with the command to "go and make disciples of all the nations," along with the comforting though enigmatic promise that Jesus somehow would be with his followers "to the end of the ages." Luke instead ends his gospel with a command to "stay" and with an intriguing hint of something else still to come, as he says to the disciples on the road to Emmaus:

> "These are my words that I spoke to you while I was still with you— that everything written about me in the law of Moses, the prophets, and the psalms must be fulfilled." Then he opened their minds to understand the scriptures, and he said to them, "Thus it is written, that the Messiah is to suffer and to rise from the dead on the third day, and that repentance and forgiveness of sins is to be proclaimed in his name to all nations, beginning from Jerusalem. You are witnesses of these things. And see, I am sending upon you what my Father promised; so

stay here in the city until you have been clothed with power from on high" (Luke 24:44–49).

"Wait," Jesus commands. A specific gift is going to be given. The full nature of that gift is only hinted at here, but clearly the disciples are told not to go yet, not until they have been "clothed with power from on high." Only then will it be time to go and be Jesus' "witnesses." So ends Luke's gospel, and so begins the Acts of the Apostles.

The book of Acts opens with Luke's introductory greeting to his reader/patron, Theophilus. Here he summarizes his first account in which he "wrote about all that Jesus did and taught from the beginning" and goes on to reiterate in slightly different words what he previously said at the end of the gospel:

> While staying with them, he ordered them not to leave Jerusalem, but to wait there for the promise of the Father. "This," he said, "is what you have heard from me; for John baptized with water, but you will be baptized with the Holy Spirit not many days from now" (1:1,4–5).

Now he is more specific about the nature of the promised gift: "You will be baptized with the Holy Spirit." The timing, also, is not some vague "forever and ever" or "to the end of the ages," for it is clearly stated that this baptism will occur "not many days from now." There is no prolonged interim period, no sabbatical for these closest friends of Jesus. There is promise, and fairly soon there is fulfillment and accompanying action. It quickly becomes clear why this book would soon become known as the Acts of the Apostles, for though it contains many lengthy speeches and sermons,, it really is a book of action, movement, and progress. Things are never dull in Acts. Following the fulfillment of Jesus' promise in Acts 2, the pace of the narrative conveys the sometimes exhilarating, sometimes harrowing, but always frenetic life of the early church and its leaders, the apostles.

Sent Ones

The Greek word *apostolos* is an important word for Luke, who uses it more than any other New Testament writer, most often in the plural, describing those twelve disciples whom Jesus calls out of the multitudes to be his closest companions. *Apostolos* means "one who is sent

Apostolos means "one who is sent (forth)" or, more simply, "sent one."

(forth)" or, more simply, "sent one." As with most of the key moments of decision in Luke's writings, Jesus' selection of the Twelve followed a night of prayer (Luke 6:12–16):

> And when day came, he called his disciples and chose twelve of them, whom he also named apostles: Simon, whom he named Peter, and his brother Andrew, and James, and John, and Philip, and Bartholomew, and Matthew, and Thomas, and James son of Alphaeus, and Simon, who was called the Zealot, and Judas son of James, and Judas Iscariot, who became a traitor.

Their number recalls the twelve tribes of Israel and the twelve sons of Jacob for whom the tribes are named. Of the Twelve, we are told that at least four were Galilean fishermen (the two pairs of siblings), one was a tax collector (Levi/Matthew), and one was most likely a member of a political party committed to the overthrow of the occupying Roman Empire (Simon the Zealot). Most, if not all, lived their entire lives in that small, neglected corner of the empire. None had Greek names and the likelihood is that Aramaic, not Greek, was their native tongue. They were provincial in their experience and in their vision, and yet to these unlikely candidates Jesus gave "power and authority over all demons and to cure diseases" and commissioned them "to proclaim the kingdom of God and to heal" (Luke. 9:1–2). Proclamation accompanied by deeds of power—this was to be their apostolic work. This is what these "sent ones" were sent to do. But how would they learn to do this work? What would be their instruction guide?

For Luke, the answer is not a "what" but a "who." Jesus himself is both the prototype and the living exemplar of all that his apostles were called to be. Between their initial selection in Luke 6 and their official commissioning in Luke 9, these "sent ones" walked with Jesus and witnessed all that he said and did. If we go back two chapters before their selection, we see how Jesus himself is the prime "sent one." In a tale unique to this evangelist, we find Jesus at the inauguration of his ministry in his hometown synagogue, reading Isaiah 61: "The Spirit of the Lord God is upon me. . . ." This prophecy clearly links the proclamation of good news with acts of power and liberation (Luke 4:18). At the conclusion of the reading, Jesus declares to a stunned congregation that he himself is the fulfillment of Isaiah's prophecy, the much-anticipated "servant of the Lord," the ambassador sent by God. Noting his hearers' astonishment, Jesus goes on to expand the notion of the kind of people to whom God's sent ones are sent (4:26–29), including the prophet Elijah's ministry to the widow of Zarephath in Sidon and Elisha's healing of Naaman the Syrian, both outsiders to Israel. Apostles are sent to outsiders as well as insiders. In a literal cliffhanger ending to the story, Luke points out that the hometown response to Jesus' words is both immediate and overwhelmingly negative: "They were all filled with rage" (4:28), enough to try to hurl Jesus off a cliff, only to have him move calmly away through their midst.

In Luke's gospel, Jesus not only understands himself as God's "sent one," but recognizes that such a ministry involves moving beyond the familiar and the comfortable. This is a constant motif in the gospel, as Jesus again and again reaches out to the marginal ones of his time: women and children, servants and slaves, Samaritans and Romans, and those considered to be "sinners." All this the apostles witness as they follow Jesus in the time between their calling and their commissioning. Yet they often do not seem to get it, as several stories in Luke show them unable to heal a demon-possessed child (9:36–42), arguing amongst themselves about who is greatest (9:46–48), jealous of others who are successful (9:49–50), and even vengeful following a failed mission to a Samaritan village (9:51–56). It is little wonder that Luke soon introduces another group, seventy workers whom Jesus also sends out in pairs, a story that is, once again, unique to Luke (10:1ff).

All this brings us back to Acts 1, where Jesus speaks once more to his sent ones before his departure. He bids them to stay, to stay in Jerusalem, "to wait for the promise of the Father." And what is the response of the apostles to this command to stay? "So when they had come together, they asked him, 'Lord, is this the time when you will restore the kingdom to Israel?" (1:5). We cannot blame the apostles for thinking that this is the goal toward which they have been moving. We can, however, admit that their question shows a touch of naiveté—they still do not get it! They are still thinking of Israel's hope and consolation, still content to stay with the familiar and the comfortable. Jesus' reply should not surprise us: "It is not for you to know the times or periods that the Father has set." He does not say, "That is a really dumb question," but he does challenge them to move them from thinking that this is the happy ending to their journey to accepting that this is just the beginning of a new journey, or at least a new phase in their journey. Throughout the gospel Jesus has set his face towards Jerusalem, even when the apostles tried to dissuade him. Now, just when they are getting comfortable there, he explains that Jerusalem is not the finish line but the starting point. It is time for the sent ones to be sent out: "But you will receive power when the Holy Spirit has come upon you; and you will be my witnesses in Jerusalem, in all Judea and Samaria, and to the ends of the earth" (1:8).

In a scene reminiscent of the first Easter morning, Jesus' friends stand staring at the sky following his departure, as if he might change his mind and suddenly come back. Finally, an angel, like some heavenly traffic cop, tells them to stop loitering, there's nothing more to see, move along. And so they go—back to Jerusalem, back to "the room upstairs where they were staying" (1:13). In a very brief amount of space here at the start of Acts, Luke has made clear that this new book is not simply a repeat of what has come before. Those who formerly were the supporting actors in the divine drama are now the leads, and they have been given a monumental task that will take them to locales both familiar and exotic. They will be Jesus' *marturoi*, but not simply in the sense of dying for a cause (though all of them will face possible death in the book, and one will actually perish). *Marturoi* is a plural form of *martus*, which literally means "witness," and was used in Jesus' time both in legal and non-legal contexts. Rather, they are to be martyrs by bearing witness to Jesus' life, death, and resurrection. The Acts of the Apostles could just as easily have been titled "The Way of the Witnesses." But what happens when one witness, one apostle, goes rogue and does the unthinkable, and then dies himself? What do you do when your team has ended one part of the race, not yet begun the new part, and realize that you are actually one person short?

> *Marturoi* is a plural form of *martus,* which literally means "witness," and was used in Jesus' time both in legal and non-legal contexts.

And Then There Were Twelve

The remainder of Acts 1 consists of a highly practical dilemma for Peter and his colleagues. Back in that upper room, the apostles devote themselves to prayer, and not they alone, but a group that includes Mary, the mother of Jesus, and his brothers, and other unnamed persons. Altogether the group numbers "one hundred and twenty" (1:14–15). Numbers are rarely arbitrary in Scripture. Certainly, for Luke this is a significant number, insofar as it is the traditional number needed to form a new synagogue community with its own governing council. Luke is certainly not suggesting that the apostles are forming a wholly independent group, for at the end of his gospel it is clear that in the days following Jesus' departure the apostles are "continually in the temple" (Luke 24:53). Their Jewish heritage is immensely important to the apostles; it is evident in their question to Jesus in 1:6 about the restoration of the kingdom of Israel and then in the numbering of their group at one hundred and twenty. It is as if Luke wants to be absolutely clear that this new movement is continuous with, and grows out of, their Jewish roots. Likewise, the importance of that Jewish heritage is clear in their story that comprises the remainder of Acts 1.

The passage begins with the words "In those days" (1:15), a phrase Luke often uses as a transition marker, to note that something new is coming that readers should notice. Jesus is gone. His departure has left a vacuum of leadership. Now, in the move back to Jerusalem, Peter suddenly takes the reins of this new messianic community and Luke immediately calls attention to the empty slot in their roster left by the death of the traitor Judas. The Twelve are now the eleven. Again, numbers have meaning, and the number twelve is one of the most important, reminding the reader of the twelve tribes of Israel and the twelve sons of Jacob for whom the tribes are named. To a group that only recently asked the Risen Lord about the restoration of Israel, it appears crucial to fill the vacancy and return to the full contingent of twelve apostles before the fulfillment of Jesus' promise of the Spirit. All this Peter explains in what is the first of several lengthy speeches in Acts.

It should be noted that, although the identified speaker is Peter and his audience the upper room community, this and all the speeches we find in Acts reveal Luke's editorial hand. This is evident in the consistent evangelistic formula, or kerygma, in each instance, a formula that summarizes Jesus' ministry from the baptism by John through his crucifixion and death to his resurrection and ascension (1:21–22). This kerygma would eventually be summarized in the church's eucharist acclamation: "Christ has died, Christ is risen, Christ will come again." Luke's editorial work is also noticeable in his translation or explanation of phrases or customs that, while familiar to the original speaker and his audience, would have been unknown to Luke's late first-century readers. An example of this is found in 1:19, "so that the field was called in their language Hakeldama, that is, Field of Blood." Such an explanation, especially regarding "their language," would have made no sense coming out of Peter's mouth. Indeed, Old Testament quotations in Acts are usually taken not from the Hebrew texts, but from the Septuagint, which the Galilean fisherman Simon Peter would certainly not have understood, but which was the familiar version of the scriptures for Luke and his readers. The Septuagint, literally meaning "seventy," was the Greek translation of the Hebrew Scriptures put together, according to tradition, by seventy scholars. Therefore, in reading this and subsequent speeches in Acts, it is helpful to recognize that we are hearing not only the speaker's voice, but Luke's as well.

> This kerygma would eventually be summarized in the church's eucharist acclamation: "Christ has died, Christ is risen, Christ will come again."

> The Septuagint, literally meaning "seventy," was the Greek translation of the Hebrew Scriptures put together, according to tradition, by seventy scholars.

This first speech, along with all those that follow, begins, unsurprisingly, with Scripture: "Friends, the scripture had to be fulfilled." Throughout Acts Luke emphasizes the new faith's grounding in Judaism, both through the apostles' regular participation in temple or synagogue worship and by offering continual biblical references and antecedents for their actions. In an empire where new religions are a dime a dozen, it appears quite important for Luke to underscore the fact that this is not simply one more new, unknown sectarian group. Rather, this Christ-focused community represents a legitimate development of the recognized tradition of Abraham, Moses, Deborah, and David. There needs to be twelve apostles, not eleven, because the scriptures say so. There needs to be a successor to Judas, because the scriptures say so. Even the circumstances surrounding Judas' betrayal are understood as somehow, in some way, fulfilling the biblical prophecies. Again, Luke is clear that the scriptures say so.

The fact that this first speech focuses on Judas, who was "numbered among us and was allotted his shared in this ministry" (1:17) is significant, as is the added fact that it is Peter who assumes the role of chief spokesperson for the new community. Just as Luke pointed to unlikely heroes in his gospel—women who normally had no power in ancient society, Roman centurions, even a despised Samaritan—in Acts he makes no attempt to gloss over the fact that the two primary leaders in the early church were formerly a coward and a persecutor. In contrast to Judas, who died in his sin, Peter and Paul stand as signs of hope that one does not have to be perfect to be an apostle. (As a side note, it is interesting to see in this speech a hint of Luke's traditionally designated profession as a "beloved physician" in his graphic description of Judas' disembowelment.)

What is needed to fill the apostolic seat, however, is evidence of having accompanied Jesus from the start of his ministry until his departure. An eyewitness is needed, Peter says, thereby providing physical, tangible continuity of leadership, in much the same way that the church would later understand apostolic succession. This is, of course, very different from Paul's understanding of apostleship as expressed in his letters. But it can even be argued that Peter's definition of apostleship as eyewitness is not necessarily shared by the editor, Luke. For two candidates who obviously fit the requirements are put forward, one whose full name and alias is given ("Joseph called Barsabbas, who was also known as Justus") and the one who actually is selected, quiet Matthias (1:23). I say "quiet" not because he is described as such but because, following his selection, we never hear of Matthias again. This is a little curious, since Luke makes a point of including this pre-Pentecost tale of the selection of a twelfth apostle only to ignore him completely hereafter. This is in direct contrast to other witnesses who are prominently featured in Acts, figures like Stephen, Barnabas, Philip, and, of course, Paul.

Besides the silence following Matthias' selection, the process by which he is chosen is itself intriguing. It involves prayer, which is

Klātos or "lot" refers to a pebble or bit of wood or similar item marked with the person's name and thrown with other similar objects into a container which is then shaken, so that the lot which falls out first is the one chosen.

typical of Luke, but then moves into an uncharacteristic method of casting *klātoi* or "lots" (1:26). *Klātos* or "lot" refers to a pebble or bit of wood or similar item marked with the person's name and thrown with other similar objects into a container which is then shaken, so that the lot which falls out first is the one chosen. Luke adds a bit of a play on words, as "lot" is also the word used earlier in Peter's speech to describe Judas: "For he was numbered among us and was allotted his share in this ministry." Likewise, the word appears again in the group's prayer: "Lord, you know everyone's heart. Show us which one of these two you have chosen to take the place ("lot") in this ministry and apostleship from which Judas turned aside to go to his own place" (1:25).

Even more intriguing is the fact that this pre-Pentecost process actually finds it roots back in Old Testament times as a way of determining God's will in certain decisions. Proverbs 16:33 says, "The lot is cast into the lap,/ but the decision is the LORD's alone." It will be seen how later decisions in Acts, including decisions concerning difficult or complex situations such as the inclusion of the Gentiles, will be decided in other ways—but not this one. In other words, this synagogue-like community of one hundred and twenty, governed by a council of twelve patriarchs, working and worshiping in the shadow of the Jerusalem temple, chooses as their apostolic selection process a method straight out of ancient Israel. Is this a necessary prerequisite step to the empowerment by the Spirit, or does the process speak more about the apostles' longing for the restoration of the kingdom of Israel? Luke does not offer an easy answer to this query, but has given us much to consider about what it means to be an apostle.

The Last Word

Indeed, Luke's last word in this pre-Pentecost section of Acts is literally "apostle," as it is mentioned that Matthias, the one chosen by the casting of lots, is "added to the eleven apostles" (1:26). This prologue to the evangelist's second volume, sandwiched between Jesus' commissioning of his witnesses and their empowerment by the Spirit, has concerned itself with the call and definition of apostleship, and so it might well be our task to consider once more Jesus' words on the subject.

"You will receive power," he tells them, "and you will be my witnesses to the ends of the earth." Jesus, the apostolic exemplar, calls his closest friends to follow in the way that he himself has shown. To be an apostle is to be a witness even as he was a witness, to go to parts unknown, unfamiliar, uncomfortable, even as he did, to set their faces away from Jerusalem even as he had once set his face towards it. Yes, Jesus' commission at the start of Acts makes clear that to be an apostle is to go out, but we must remember that before going it is important to *stay*, to wait for the power of the Spirit. As the opening collect for mission says, it is God who "raises up in this and every land evangelists and heralds of the kingdom." Whether we number eleven or twelve or seventy or one hundred and twenty, whether we feel afraid or ready, we are always to remember that God's "sent ones" are empowered by God to do God's work in God's world. Whatever acts of the apostles may follow, they are always grounded in the calling of God, the model of Jesus, and the power of the Spirit.

CHAPTER 2

Apostolic Concord

Shed abroad this gift throughout the world by the preaching of the Gospel, that it may reach to the ends of the earth.

COLLECT FOR THE DAY OF PENTECOST, THE BOOK OF COMMON PRAYER

A wise but mischievous Senior Warden once said that if, as several church members proclaimed with great hyperbole, there had been a "golden age" in the life of the parish, he must have blinked and missed it. The compilers of the biblical canon seem to agree with such a sentiment. The Hebrew scriptures begin with the recounting of an idyllic time in humanity's story, a paradise on earth, the Garden of Eden. Interestingly, this tale of a golden age occupies but a tiny space in the Old Testament canon, as contrasted with the multi-volume account of the wanderings in the wilderness and the subsequent struggles to claim the Promised Land. Similarly, the golden age of David's united monarchy represents only a brief amount of time, as contrasted with the ensuing centuries of divided houses and the Babylonian exile. Following the reigns of David and his son Solomon, the united kingdom split into the northern land of Israel and the southern land of Judah, each with their own sets of rulers.

> Following the reigns of David and his son Solomon, the united kingdom split into the northern land of Israel and the southern land of Judah, each with their own sets of rulers.

Even so, the two-thousand-year-old history of the church began with a golden age of its own, a time when the gospel was proclaimed and mighty works of power performed, when believers were all of one heart and soul in apostolic concord, and they shared all that they have with one another. Not surprisingly, this golden age—like all others—did not last long, but it stands forever as a Camelot and, even more, as a foretaste of the heavenly kingdom. And it all began with Pentecost.

Harvest Time

We are so accustomed to thinking of the Day of Pentecost as a Christian feast that we can forget that it existed as a Jewish feast many centuries before the church inherited it. Indeed, it is the second of the three great Jewish feasts, celebrated fifty days after the Passover and the offering of first-fruits. The term Pentecost means "fiftieth day." According to the book of Leviticus, on this feast day the people brought to the priest the sheaf representing the "first fruits" of what they hoped would be a good harvest. The priest would raise the sheaf on the day after the Sabbath, and a lamb would be offered as sacrifice. And from the day after the sabbath, from the day on which you bring the sheaf of the elevation-offering, you shall count off seven weeks; they shall be complete. You shall count until the day after the seventh sabbath, fifty days; then you shall present an offering of new grain to the LORD (Lev. 23:15–16).

> The term Pentecost means "fiftieth day."

Thus Pentecost, or the Feast of Weeks, is also appropriately known as the Festival of Harvest, for it points to the fullness of what was foreseen in the first-fruits seven weeks previously.

Pentecost also commemorated the giving of the Decalogue at Mount Sinai, the Mosaic law that would help form the basis of the community that had proceeded out of Egypt. Unlike Passover, this was not to be a quiet family commemoration, but a time when all the people would come together for a brief time to renew their connection to God and to one another, to recall the ties of both liberty

> And from the day after the sabbath, from the day on which you bring the sheaf of the elevation- offering, you shall count off seven weeks; they shall be complete. You shall count until the day after the seventh sabbath, fifty days; then you shall present an offering of new grain to the LORD. (Lev. 23:15–16)

and law that bound them as one. Finally, as a fascinating and often overlooked aspect of the feast, Leviticus reiterates an earlier divine challenge that the people were required by God to leave some of the gleanings at the time of harvest, so that the poor might be able to collect that which had been left behind for their own sustenance (Lev. 19:19). Even here—perhaps especially here—in this celebration of the much anticipated harvest, in this feast of the community of the faithful, the people were charged to remember others in need. Their generosity would give life and hope to outsiders as well.

In the centuries between those wilderness wanderings and the coming of the church in Acts, Israel's fortunes rose and fell many times. With the establishment of the monarchy came the creation of the temple in Jerusalem, followed in turn by the division of the kingdom and the temple's eventual destruction. Centuries of exile were followed by a return to the land and the construction of a second temple. This, however, was no second golden age. "Herod's temple," as this second one would be known, was smaller and less impressive than its predecessor, and Herod was no David, merely a puppet ruler for the Roman occupiers. It is little wonder that many of the people living in Palestine at the time of Jesus were looking for a messiah, for a Son of David who could restore what had been lost. They were looking for the harvest when the seeds of God's reign would burst forth in glory.

These multiple layers of meaning surrounding the feast of Pentecost would not have been lost on the many Jewish pilgrims and proselytes who made their way to Jerusalem and the temple. They came with their frustrations about the present situation and their anxieties about the future, but they still came. And so did the Spirit.

Like the Rush of a Violent Wind

While the festival visitors found their way to the temple grounds, the apostles and their closest companions were already in Jerusalem, still huddled together in a closed room. Whether in hope or in fear, they did as they had been told; they waited and prayed. Then, as Acts 2:2–3 vividly states "And suddenly from heaven there came a sound like the rush of a violent wind, and it filled the entire house where they were sitting. Divided tongues, as of fire, appeared among them, and a tongue rested on each of them." The images are provocative, suggesting several precedents in the Hebrew scriptures. One story that might come to mind involves the prophet Elijah, that archetype of the lone, courageous champion, standing in the breach for God against four hundred pagan priests. But Elijah was human, and in the face of pressure, his famed valor gave way to utter trepidation. In a cave far from the frontlines of the prophetic mission, Elijah hid and waited for God to answer his pleas. In a scene that today seems cinematic, the prophet heard the sound of a great *pneuma,* or wind, only to realize that God was not in the wind. The Greek pneuma can mean either "wind" or "spirit," and was usually used in the Septuagint to translate the Hebrew *ruach.* Following this wind came both an earthquake and a fire, but God's presence was only sensed when there came a slight breeze like the cool, fresh air of morning, or what the King James Bible calls "a still small voice" (1 Kings 19:9–12).

> The Greek pneuma can mean either "wind" or "spirit," and was usually used in the Septuagint to translate the Hebrew *ruach.*

From the beginning of creation, moreover, the book of Genesis declares that it was God's wind that "swept over the face of the waters" and God's breath that gave life to the first human being (Gen.1:2; 2:7). The psalms proclaim that God "brings out the wind from his storehouses" (Ps. 135:7), even as Proverbs speaks of God gathering "the wind in the hollow of the hand" (Prov. 30:4). The Hebrew Scriptures are clear that God is the source of both the mighty wind and the breath of life. It is on this rich Old Testament imagery that Luke draws to describe a new act of God in the life of God's people, as Jesus' followers found the room in which they waited suddenly filled with a violent wind, followed by the quiet, profound presence of God in the form of tongues of fire. In power and in intimacy, the apostles were filled with the Holy Spirit and sent forth.

A Very Good Beginning

In just a few verses, the story of Jesus' followers takes a quantum leap forward. Following the descent of the Holy Spirit, the formerly timid apostles suddenly turn into preaching dynamos. The results are remarkable—and controversial. This group of unlearned individuals is proclaiming the story of Jesus in several different languages, while onlookers question how this can be possible and even whether the apostles are drunk. Right there at the start, the church is having to explain itself! The speech that Simon Peter gives in response draws his Jewish audience right back to the scriptures. He quotes first from Joel 2:28–32, a passage filled not with words of comfort but rather apocalyptic imagery about "the last days," a time of portents and prophecies when the Spirit would be poured out "on all flesh" and everyone who would call on the name of the Lord "shall be saved." Then, evoking the great King David, Peter goes on to convey how David himself pointed towards a still greater Messiah, who was none other than "this Jesus whom you crucified." Then the same crowd, who only a short time before has accused the apostles of being drunk, now beg Peter to explain what they should do in response to his message, asking "What shall we do?" With a dramatic flourish, Peter responds with what in later centuries would be best described as an altar call, calling on the people to repent and be baptized in the name of Jesus, "and you will receive the gift of the Holy Spirit" (2:38).

The people respond dramatically, with three thousand converts added to that small band of previously timid followers. The day ended quite differently than it had begun. With words that eventually would form part of the church's baptismal covenant, the remainder of Acts 2 offers a memorable summary of the communal life that resulted, as members "devoted themselves to the apostles' teaching and fellowship, to the breaking of bread, and the prayers." The apostles displayed "signs and wonders" and their followers "had all things in common," selling their possessions and sharing with one another, even as new members were daily added to their number. The Spirit has come. The fearful have found power. A community is born.

It is a well-known adage that any change is threatening to a system. The system that was first-century Palestinian Judaism was already threatened for its very existence by the visible presence of its Roman overlords. Keeping a low profile became a priority for many Jewish residents. Some—especially those who cooperated directly with, or worked for, the Romans—even thrived, though often at the expense of cordial relations with their fellow Jews. Whatever their individual outcomes, the people knew that collectively theirs was a very precarious situation, with the Romans holding the key to their survival. To many Jewish leaders in Jerusalem, the last thing they needed was a small sect babbling on about another messiah to free them from Rome's tyranny. So the reaction of the leadership to the apostles' newfound success was immediate. Scholars note that from the period immediately before Jesus' birth until the destruction of Jerusalem in 70 CE, over thirty would-be messiahs came and went, with their followers.

It was a healing miracle that ignited the outburst. It happens while Peter and John are on their way to the temple, Luke's reminder to his readers that the apostles are still very much faithful Jews. The fact that they are now convinced that Jesus was their anticipated messiah does not change their foundational commitment to the religious practices in which they had been reared. As is evident in the first several chapters of Acts, all their proclamation and miracles and new life together occurred in the shadow of the temple. On the way to prayer Peter and John encounter a beggar lame from birth. In another delightfully dramatic moment from Luke, Peter faces the beggar, looks him in the eye, and says, "I have no silver or gold, but what I have I give to you; in the name of Jesus Christ of Nazareth, stand up and walk" (3:6). And the lame beggar did just that. Like Jesus, the apostles not only spoke with power, but performed deeds of power in Jesus' name. The story might have remained a private affair, but Luke notes that the man went out and told everyone, whereupon Peter followed up with another evangelistic sermon. And "many of those who heard the word believed, and they numbered about five thousand" (4:4). His success is a threat to the status quo.

So when word of what happened reaches the Sanhedrin, they convene a gathering and bring Peter and John before them, demanding, "By what power or by what name do you do this?" Sanhedrin is the Greek word for council, literally "sitting together," to designate a judicial and administrative body. In the gospels the Sanhedrin is made up

> Scholars note that from the period immediately before Jesus' birth until the destruction of Jerusalem in 70 CE, over thirty would-be messiahs came and went, with their followers.

> Sanhedrin is the Greek word for council, literally "sitting together," to designate a judicial and administrative body. In the gospels the Sanhedrin is made up of local elites and, together with the chief priests, is often depicted as the center of hostility to Jesus' teaching.

of local elites and, together with the chief priests, is often depicted as the center of hostility to Jesus' teaching.

Luke makes it clear that as Peter responds, he does so "filled with the Holy Spirit" (4:7–8). The address that follows is no apology or excuse for the healing that started the commotion, but rather a bold affirmation of the gospel message. The religious leaders are dumbfounded. Between the obvious result of the healing itself and the impressive speech of these uneducated, ordinary fishermen, the council simply admonishes and threatens them, and then lets them go. The two apostles return to their companions and together pray with such fervent power that "the place in which they had gathered together was shaken" (4:31). There would be much opposition to come in Acts, and here we see the formula that will become familiar: a good work is performed, the threatened religious leaders or insiders oppose or arrest the disciples, those disciples offer a faithful defense of the gospel, and outsiders come to faith.

Following this report of the healing and reactions to it, Luke offers another summary of the believers' common life: "Now the whole group of those who believed were of one heart and soul, and no one claimed private ownership of any possessions, but everything they owned was held in common" (4:32). This small but fast-growing Jewish sectarian movement was one that emphasized interdependence among its members. In this system, the apostles act as leaders in more than one sphere; not only are they the chief preachers and workers of deeds of power, but it is also at their feet that people lay the proceeds of their sales of property to be "distributed to each as any had need" (4:35). One particular landowner who did just that, bringing the proceeds of a field he sold to the apostles, was a Levite from Cyprus named Joseph, who would become far better known by the nickname the apostles gave him: Barnabas. The name Barnabas literally means something like "son (*bar*) of prophecy (*nebu'ah*)" or perhaps just "son of Nebo," but Luke also makes clear that the apostles viewed him as a "son of encouragement."

> The name Barnabas literally means something like "son (*bar*) of prophecy (*nebu'ah*)" or perhaps just "son of Nebo," but Luke also makes clear that the apostles viewed him as a "son of encouragement."

A Chilling Tale

Shortly after we are introduced to Barnabas, Luke provides an unusual and unnerving tale, one that provides a contrast to generous Barnabas in the persons of Ananias and Sapphira. Here is a couple who have agreed to sell a piece of property but then gave only a portion of the proceeds to the apostles, secretly holding back the rest. In the Book of Common Prayer, a prayer used at the beginning of every eucharist says, "Almighty God, to you all hearts are open, all desires known, and from you no secrets are hid. . . ." Ananias soon learns how true this is. For Peter challenges him, noting that the property and its proceeds were his to do with as he desired, but now it is the intention of his heart that God is judging: "How is it that you have contrived this deed in your heart? You did not lie to us but to God!" (5:4). At once Ananias falls down dead, and a group of young men wrap up his body and bury it.

Three hours later, Ananias's widow Sapphira arrives and is also confronted by Peter. Even more than the previous scene, this encounter has an almost film noir quality to it. Luke the "director" presents a memorable image as the apostle questions Sapphira about the price of the land she and Ananias have sold. Whether she is suspicious or not, the guilty woman looks at Peter and responds with a lie. You can almost hear the resonating minor chords in the background as Peter's words reach Sapphira: "Look, the feet of those who have buried your husband are at the door, and they will carry you out" (5:9). The epilogue to the story declares that "great fear seized the whole church" (5:9–11). Is it any wonder?

This narrative is indeed jarring, especially after hearing about how wonderful things were in the believers' idyllic community. But perhaps that is exactly what Luke is trying to tell us. Again, there never has been a perfect golden age. As the book of Genesis reminds us, even in the Garden of Eden there dwelled a serpent. Indeed, the unhappy account of Ananias and Sapphira almost echoes the story of Adam and Eve's fall. The community of believers in Jerusalem was wonderful, but it was not paradise, and Acts makes certain that we do not forget this. At the same time, this tale makes the contributions of Barnabas and other newcomers yet to appear all the more remarkable.

Success . . . to a Point

After that unsettling interlude, Luke's familiar rhythm of miracle, opposition, and growth begins again, starting with "Now many signs and wonders were done among the people through the apostles." (v. 12). This is an appropriate place to take note of some key points about the work of the Twelve in these early chapters in Acts.

First, the apostles clearly exercise a ministry of proclamation and power to which they were earlier commissioned in the Gospel of Luke, but most failed to perform. Apostolic proclamation in Acts takes the form of two public addresses—Peter's sermon on the day of Pentecost (2:14–36) and his words to the crowd after healing a blind beggar (3:12–26)—and his testimony before the Jewish rulers and elders (4:8–12; 5:29–32). In Peter's sermons, the implicit message of Jesus' inaugural sermon in the synagogue about the Servant of the Lord becomes an explicit pronouncement about Jesus the crucified and risen Messiah. Along with proclamation come deeds of power. The casting out of demons in Acts 5:16 is particularly significant, since their failure to do so earlier had been a sore point for the Twelve in Luke's gospel, as others accomplished what they appeared unable to do. Furthermore, even as a hemorrhaging woman once touched the hem of Jesus' cloak and was healed, so in Acts 5:15 the sick are laid out in the street in order to have Peter's shadow fall on them. It is clearly a new day for the apostles after Pentecost.

Second, it is clear in these early chapters that the power behind the Twelve is the Holy Spirit, the same Spirit that anointed and empowered Jesus. With the exception of the choosing of Matthias as the twelfth disciple, there is little doubt that the words and works of the Twelve are due not to their own cleverness or ability, but to the promised Spirit of God. The result is "amazement" and some perplexity (2:12) on the part of the observers. Similarly, the bold confession of Peter and John after the healing of the lame man in Acts 3 and the apostles' defense in Acts 5 appear to fulfill Jesus' promise to the apostles while he is still teaching in the temple: "I will give you words and a wisdom that none of your opponents will be able to withstand or contradict" (21:15). Here also are strong echoes of the mixed response to Jesus following his initial, controversial message in his hometown synagogue: "All spoke well of him and were amazed at the gracious words that came from his mouth. They said, 'Is not this Joseph's son?'" The Spirit of the Lord was upon Jesus to proclaim, to heal, and to exorcise. Now that same Spirit is empowering the apostles.

Third, the Twelve experienced great results in their mission, in terms of both the numbers of their converts and their devotion to teaching and fellowship. Such passages have been cited through the centuries as a model for success for the Christian church. But their success was limited, for—and this is a crucial fourth point—all the preaching and miraculous signs of the Twelve, and all their subsequent success in those early chapters of Acts, occurred within Jerusalem, in the precincts of the temple.

After remarking how signs and wonders were done through the apostles, Acts 5:12 goes on to say, "And they were all together ("all with one accord," King James Version) in Solomon's Portico." The porch, or portico, was a covered colonnade built by Solomon in the eastern part of the original Jerusalem temple, a colonnade that survived the Babylonian invasion that destroyed the rest of the temple. The portico stood intact to the time when Herod's temple was built on the original site. It was an open space where the followers of Jesus gathered together. The specific reference to it here is another reminder that the apostles and the community that has grown up around them remain faithful Jews who esteem the traditions of their native religion and show little concern for moving beyond it. Although the Pentecost scene revealed that there was some diversity in geographical background for the believers, those who remained in Jerusalem and became part of that apostolic community constituted a fairly homogeneous group of faithful Jewish believers who are now convinced that Jesus was their long-desired Messiah. Despite Jesus' own clear call to move beyond Jerusalem "through all Judea and Samaria to the ends of the earth," there seems to be no hint of the Twelve doing anything but staying put. Their routine consisted of breaking bread in private homes while still spending time each day in the temple. The healing of a lame man occurs at the "Beautiful Gate" as Peter and John are going "up to the temple at the hour of prayer" (3:1) and, after their release from the authorities, the Twelve return daily to the temple.

This is not to make light of the remarkable success that the apostles did experience in the first few chapters of Acts. It is important, however, to acknowledge the all-too-familiar limits of that success. As will be seen, it will take Stephen's stoning (for questioning the need for the temple, among other things) and the resulting dispersion of the believers to many places throughout the Roman Empire for Jesus' geographical challenge to be fulfilled. And even then, when the gospel does go "to the ends of the earth," Luke is unambiguous in stating that the apostles still remained in Jerusalem: "And all except the apostles were scattered throughout the countryside of Judea and Samaria" (8:1).

There is a true story of a Swiss inventor who decades ago came up with the idea of a watch that did not require winding or moveable gears. When he shared the idea with the powers that be in Swiss watch-making, they scoffed at it and said it was not really a watch at all. They did not simply say that they didn't like it; they actually denied that it fit into their parameters of what a watch is! These Swiss watchmakers were collectively extremely successful, but their own success prevented them from seeing something outside their expected view. The apostles were extremely successful, as well, but within a religious and cultural context that is above all represented by the temple in Jerusalem. We have much to celebrate about Pentecost, but if it had not been for the newcomers who, with the exception of Barnabas, are not even on the scene yet by the end of Acts 5, the Jesus movement might very well have remained a Jewish sectarian association.

A Story of Stewardship

Luke's narrative of the apostolic community places utmost importance on the role that money and material possessions play in the story. This is no surprise, as more than any of the other gospel writers Luke speaks of financial issues throughout his account of Jesus's ministry. For Luke, possessions and financial stewardship are not one aspect of the gospel message to be discussed apart from other areas of ministry such as outreach or evangelism. On the contrary, the evangelist depicts money and material goods as pervasive symbols of people's response to Christ and the Christian gospel. Indeed, in his gospel those who have experienced conversion in their lives often reflect that internal change by displaying an external modification in the ordering of their financial priorities. Zaccheus, that delightful "vertically-challenged" tax collector who climbed a sycamore tree to see Jesus, is Luke's perfect model for the converted life. There is no mention there of a formal initiation rite. Rather, following Jesus's visit to his house, Zaccheus immediately pledges to recompense those he has cheated—fourfold (Luke 19:8). For Luke, the converted life is visibly represented by a radical new approach to one's treasures. Indeed, although his gospel shares with Matthew's many of the same injunctions and stories about the danger of trusting in possessions—material not found in Mark's gospel—Luke places these otherwise disparate sayings into one long sermon in Luke 12, which offers a fairly consistent message about the danger of trusting in apparent financial security. It is particularly intriguing to note the importance of the stories that are unique to Luke, such as the tale of the younger and older brothers vying for the family inheritance and the parable of the rich man who puts all his energy and his trust into his financial preparations for the future. They suggest the foolishness of a life in which God is ignored and riches are idolized: "God said to him, 'You fool! This very night your life is being demanded of you. And the things you have prepared, whose will they be?' 21So it is with those who store up treasures for themselves but are not rich towards God" (Luke 12:20–21). In the Hebrew Scriptures, almsgiving is a tangible form of compassion, as seen in both the psalms ("Happy are those who consider the poor," 41:1) and in Proverbs ("Those who oppress the poor insult their Maker, but those who are kind to the needy honor him," 14:31). In Acts, however, Luke moves beyond almsgiving in describing the financial choices made by the new believers after the events of Pentecost. The converts immediately begin to display a radical change in life by selling their possessions and bringing the proceeds to the apostles, so that those among them in need may be aided. Luke's Old Testament precedent is Deuteronomy 15: "If there is among you anyone in need, a member of your community in any of your towns within the land that the LORD your God is giving you, do not be hard-hearted or tight-fisted toward your needy neighbor" (v. 7). In similar words, Leviticus

25:35 states: "If any of your kin fall into difficulty and become dependent on you, you shall support them." In the words of the well-known religious folk song, "And they'll know we are Christians by our love." The most powerful and visible argument for the truths the apostles proclaimed is not the deeds of power that accompany their message, but rather what Luke describes in the phrase from Acts: "There was not a needy person among them" (4:34). Miracles then and now astound and amaze, but a community that truly takes care of its own is itself a miracle.

Furthermore, the apostles are seen at the end of Acts 4 and beginning of Acts 5 as being integrally involved in the reception and distribution of those material goods. Believers like Barnabas sell their property and possessions, and lay the proceeds "at the feet" of the apostles. This phrase "at the feet" (*para tous podas*) is a significant one for Luke, who uses it to denote both a sense of devotion or reverence that the giver has for the receiver and the trustworthiness of the receiver. It is a phrase found most often in his writings; indeed, over forty-three percent of all New Testament occurrences of "feet" (*podas*) occur in Luke and Acts. It is used here to denote the entrusting of possessions to another who is deemed trustworthy, as when the witnesses at Stephen's stoning lay their cloaks "at the feet of a young man named Saul" (7:58), trusting him to watch over them. Both trust and respect are clearly conveyed in the twin instances of followers laying their money before the apostles (4:35, 37). The mention of the apostles' powerful testimony to the resurrection that precedes Luke's discussion on the sharing of possessions, actually serves to show how they exercise both spiritual and social leadership in that communal system: "With great power the apostles gave their testimony to the resurrection of the Lord Jesus, and great grace was upon them all" (v.33). Under the apostles' leadership, the gospel message is preached and the needs of all in the community are met through the distribution of funds. Whether they directly oversaw the fund or not, Luke makes it clear that it is to the apostles that financial gifts such as Barnabas' were entrusted, and then distribution made.

This will be an important point to remember while examining in the next chapter the grievances of the Hellenistic widows. For now, we see that Barnabas and many other followers sold what they owned, gave of the proceeds through a system in some way involving the leadership of the Twelve, and thereby displayed a mutual care for one another, a deep sense of their interdependence. When Acts 4:32 declares that the believers were "of one heart and soul," what is actually said in the Greek is that "there was one heart and soul in the multitude of those who believed." This is more than a common purpose; it is a common life. In the same way that the presentation of the proceeds at the feet of the apostles is symbolic of an internal reality—the great reverence that the Jerusalem Christians feel toward their leaders—even so their outward giving points to their awareness of the interwoven nature of their lives in Christ. In his first letter to the Corinthians, Paul uses the image of the human body to describe the same kind of Christian unity that is depicted here by Luke in story form. The believers in Jerusalem are stewards not simply of finances, but of one another. Of course, as noted already, there are limits to their pastoral and financial interdependence, as the golden age of the Jerusalem believers is about to pass away.

CHAPTER 3

Apostolic Challenge

*We give you thanks, O Lord of glory, for
the example of the first martyr Stephen,
who looked up to heaven and prayed for
his persecutors to your Son Jesus Christ.*

COLLECT FOR THE FEAST OF ST. STEPHEN,
THE BOOK OF COMMON PRAYER

From the very start of Acts 6, a noticeable change begins
to take place in Luke's account. The opening phrase in
6:1—"now during those days" or "and in those days"—is a
transition phrase often employed by Luke to signal a new
phase in his narrative. It is a phrase he uses far more often
than any other New Testament writer. Consider that familiar opening to the Christmas story in Luke 2:1, "In those
days a decree went out from Emperor Augustus that all the
world should be registered," or Jesus' selection of the apostles in Luke 6:12, "Now during those days he went out to
the mountain to pray." We can even return to Acts 1:15, in
which Matthias was chosen to fill the missing apostolic
twelfth spot, "In those days Peter stood up among the
believers." As in these other passages, we have a watershed
moment. All has seemed idyllic in the apostolic community, and yet now problems begin to arise. The "one heart
and soul" of Acts 4:32 has given way to a dispute between
the "Hellenists" and the "Hebrews" that is to have far-
reaching consequences.

The terms Luke uses here leave later readers like us with
more confusion than clarity regarding both the exact

nature of the conflict and the identity of the players involved. Who are these Hellenists and Hebrews, why are they fighting, and what solution will the apostles offer in response? Perhaps most important, does their solution work or not? Far from being purely academic, these questions can lead us to understand the significance of that first intra-church quarrel, and how it was, in many ways, the prototype for subsequent conflicts that would plague the community of believers even to our own time.

"Not Like Us"

Whatever else is going on in Acts 6, one thing is clear: the dispute involves two groups of people who view themselves as very different from one another. The Hellenists Luke mentions are not Gentiles, but rather Jewish Christians from outside Palestine, much like Barnabas, the Levite from Cyprus introduced earlier. As suggested by the name Luke gives these newcomers, "Hellenists," their first language was most likely Greek, not Aramaic, and their Bible was probably the Septuagint, the Greek translation of Hebrew Scripture. Because they came from outside Palestine, the Jerusalem temple might very well have been less of a focal point. The bottom line is that these newcomers as a group are viewed, and view themselves, as set apart from the so-called Hebrews. In fact, the Hellenists are now claiming that they have been treated unjustly, as their widows are getting less than their fair share of either food or funds. The latter makes greater sense in light of all that has just been said at the end of Acts 4 about community members selling their property and laying down the proceeds at the feet of the apostles. Perhaps the idyllic community of Acts 2 and 4 is not quite as harmonious as previously implied.

The likelier scenario is that the introduction of newcomers who are perceived as different from the insiders is itself a problematic situation. It is not that Luke's statements about the loving, sharing community of faith at the end of Acts 4 are inaccurate; they simply reflect a time when the community was more homogenous. Some newcomers, like Barnabas, somehow bridged the gap and were accepted into the group; others, obviously, were not. Then, as now, people who were "not like us" were viewed with some suspicion. Although there were indeed Jewish proselytes, Israel's mission has not previously been focused on evangelism and the inclusion of newcomers. Instead, the struggles they faced led the ancient Israelites to develop laws and traditions that would preserve them and their heritage. They came to understand themselves not only as the chosen people of God, but also as a people separate from outsiders and outside influences. To be a part of Israel meant being set apart from others.

It is not that these Hellenist newcomers in Acts 6 are true outsiders, like the Gentiles, but neither are they really part of the close-knit community described earlier. And so they complain of unequal treatment, as their widows were being neglected in the community's daily distribution of material goods. The word "complaining," taken from the Greek word *gogguzo,* is actually rendered in the King James Version as "murmuring." This is noteworthy, for again and again in the wilderness accounts of ancient Israel, it was said that the people "murmured" against God and Moses, often because of a lack of food or water. The word also turns up in Luke's gospel, as the Pharisees and their scribes complain about Jesus eating with "sinners" (5:30; 15:2; 19:7), spending quality time with those who were viewed, at best, as second-class believers. Now, in Luke's plot twist, it is not the Pharisees who are murmuring but fellow disciples, at their perceived treatment as second-class followers of Jesus.

The response of the apostles is quite fascinating, and not necessarily as helpful as is commonly assumed. They did not offer a remedy directly, but instead challenged the congregation—or, implicitly, the complaining Hellenist members of the congregation—to choose "seven men of good standing, full of the Spirit and of wisdom" to fulfill the task of serving tables (6:3). The Greek word *diakōnos,* from which we have the word "deacon," literally means "table server."

> The Greek word *diakōnos,* from which we have the word "deacon," literally means "table server."

Modern readers may be puzzled at the job requirements for what appears at first sight to be a menial task, but this appointment may be interpreted as more than simply pragmatic. While their work is usually considered simply an extension of the Twelve's own ministry, it is worth noting that Peter and his comrades clearly differentiate between the two. Both tasks, that of the seven and that of the twelve, are designated as *diak_nía,* or service, but one refers to "serving tables" and the other to "serving the word." Earlier the twelve had in some way overseen distribution for the whole community even as they went about proclaiming the Good News (4.35). Now there seems to be a shift, as they choose to delegate the responsibility of distribution to seven others. Whether these seven will be administrators over all distribution or just advocates for fellow Hellenists remains unclear; what is clear is that responsibility has been passed on.

If we go back further in Acts, we will recall that "in those days" Peter addressed the disciples concerning the need for a twelfth apostle to fill the place left empty by Judas. The key requirement to be an apostle and witness, Peter asserted, was that the person had to have accompanied Jesus "from the baptism of John until the day when he was taken up from us" (1:21–22). In other words, an insider was needed to replace an insider. Now, in Acts 6, we see a similar arrangement as the apostles recommend that "insiders" from among the Hellenists be appointed to respond to the complaints arising from within that system. Unlike Barnabas, the names of all seven appointees here are Greek: Stephen, meaning "crown"; Philip, or "lover of horses"; Prochorus, "leader of the chorus"; Nicanor, meaning "conqueror"; Timon, "honorable"; Parmenas, "constancy"; and Nicolaus, "victory of the people" and specifically marked out as "a proselyte of Antioch." Although this decision "pleased the whole community" (6:5), it is interesting to note that, intentionally or otherwise, the apostles' decision actually perpetuates the distinction between the two groups, the Hebrews and the Hellenists. Certainly, the Hellenists' widows now had advocates from among their own system, but was the community as a whole any more integrated by this solution?

Although the spotlight quickly turns to the first of the seven, Stephen, it is important that we not leave Luke's brief account of the first church conflict too hastily. Similar conflicts will continue to arise throughout the centuries in so many subsequent tensions among the faithful. There is no evidence here of a specific doctrinal

> Unlike Barnabas, the names of all seven appointees here are Greek: Stephen, meaning "crown"; Philip, or "lover of horses"; Prochorus, "leader of the chorus"; Nicanor, meaning "conqueror"; Timon, "honorable"; Parmenas, "constancy"; and Nicolaus, "victory of the people" and specifically marked out as "a proselyte of Antioch."

disagreement between the Hebrews and the Hellenists. No, the crucial issue is not disagreement, but a disconnect between the two groups, an apparent lack of appreciation of the tremendous gifts that the unfamiliar newcomers can offer the community and perhaps a touch of fear about what it would mean to open the door fully to those who did not have the same obvious devotion to the temple and the Hebrew traditions. The Jerusalem believers who continued their daily temple worship did welcome these newcomers, but still left a bit of a buffer zone between themselves and the newcomers by appointing the Seven to oversee the latter. The apostles' decision did allow the door to crack open a bit; now Stephen will blow that door off its hinges.

Stephen the Martyr

It is the longest sermon in the book of Acts, fifty-three verses in all, certainly the longest one-point sermon in the New Testament. Significantly, it comes from the mouth of a Hellenist leader, not one of the apostles. Stephen is one of those deacons assigned to table service while the Twelve focus on proclamation, yet immediately we see him doing apostolic, not diaconal, work: "Stephen, full of grace and power, did great wonders and signs among the people" (6:8). The phrase used here, *terata kai sāmeia* ("wonders and signs"), is the same employed earlier to describe the work of the apostles: "Awe came upon everyone, because many [*terata kai sāmeia*] were being done by the apostles" (2:43). Stephen is now doing the work of the apostles among the people. His actions draw the attention of other non-locals, people from Cyrene, Alexandria, Cilicia, and Asia— opponents who belonged to what was known as the synagogue of the Freedmen. There is still considerable debate about the exact identity of these *liberti*, as the Romans called them, but they are thought to have been either naturalized foreigners or freed slaves, or perhaps even Jews who had been granted Roman citizenship like Saul of Tarsus. Whoever they were, they didn't like Stephen, although "they could not withstand the wisdom and the Spirit with which he spoke" (6:10).

So these opponents use a more indirect approach, instigating others to accuse Stephen of blasphemy "against Moses and God." The devious nature of their attack is underscored in the King James Version, which instead of "instigate" uses the archaic word "suborn" to translate the Greek *hupobállō*. By "suborning" others, these opponents train them in what they are to say and then somehow hire or pay them to do so. These "suborned" others were nothing more than mouthpieces for those freedmen who were unable or unwilling themselves to go up against Stephen. Against Stephen the martyr—the witness—his enemies set up "false witnesses" to accuse him: "'This man never stops saying things against this holy place and the law; [14]for we have heard him say that this Jesus of Nazareth* will destroy this place and will change the customs that Moses handed on to us'" (6:13–14). Their strategy may rightly convey a sense of déjà vu, for in the gospels a similar line of attack is used against Jesus himself.

As his trial begins before the high priest, Stephen makes his formal response to the accusations against him with an epic summary of the history of Israel, beginning with God's promise to Abraham, the father of faith, and continuing through Israel's enslavement by Pharaoh, the Exodus, the years with Moses in the wilderness to David's reign. The common thread in all of it is the lack of a need for the temple. The ancestors were sojourners, and God was with them on the journey. The tabernacle that they carried with them was enough, and it was not until Solomon that the more permanent structure was built in Jerusalem. Stephen closes with a sharp contrast between the faithfulness of prophetic ancestors and the opposition of the "uncircumcised in heart and ears," and takes no chance that his audience might miss the fact that he was speaking against them: "You stiff-necked people . . . You are the ones that received the law as ordained by angels, and yet you have not kept it" (7:51–53). This rebuke is not the testimony of a defendant, but the proclamation of a prophet and martyr; not a plea that will acquit Stephen, but a confrontation that will result in his death.

The stoning of Stephen has strong, obvious parallels with the passion and death of Jesus. Even as Jesus calmly faced his enraged accusers and spoke of the Son of Man being seated at the right hand of God, so now Stephen has a vision of the Son of Man standing at the right hand of God (7:56). It is interesting to note the minor detail of "being seated" versus "standing," the former conveying rest and the latter a kind of active intercession, presumably for Stephen himself. As Stephen is being stoned, he echoes the prayer of the dying Jesus, "Receive my spirit," and asks forgiveness for his executioners (7:59–60). There is no mistaking that Luke is underscoring the fact that true witnesses of Christ not only live like Jesus, but die like him as well.

The only other detail in this tale that deserves attention is the brief aside that "the witnesses laid their coats at the feet of a young man named Saul" (v. 58). This is, of course, the future apostle and chief protagonist of the second half of Acts, but Luke's introduction of Paul is intriguing. Here we have simply one sentence mentioning a passive, albeit approving, recipient of an angry mob's cloaks, laid at his feet. What significance, if any, is there to this detail? Previously, we considered the prevalence of the term *pódas*, or "feet," in Luke's writings, noting that he uses this image of feet more than anyone else in the New Testament. Earlier Barnabas sold his lands and lay the proceeds at the feet of the apostles (4:37) and, in a macabre scene immediately after, it is the corpses of deceitful Ananias and Saphira that fall to the ground at Peter's feet (5:10). Here, however, Luke changes the pattern: It is neither the feet of Jesus nor the feet of the apostles that are the focus, but "the feet of a young man named Saul." Saul, who himself once studied diligently in Tarsus "at the feet of Gamaliel," now finds himself the recipient of the outer cloaks of the angry crowd facing Stephen. These "witnesses" entrust Saul with their mantles, and Luke notes that their trust is well-founded, as the young man approves of their killing Stephen (8:1). However, the true witness here is Stephen himself, so it may be said that it truly is his spiritual mantle that falls at Saul's feet, even as the ascending Elijah's mantle once fell down on the ground before his prophetic successor, Elisha. Certainly, most scholars of Acts speak of the Stephen story as the turning point in Luke's account of the early church. With the inclusion of Saul, however minimal his appearance at this point, it is a hint at what is to come. Of course, we must wait a little longer to see him take up Stephen's mantle and become Christ's witness to the Gentiles.

Earlier Barnabas sold his lands and lay the proceeds at the feet of the apostles (4:37) and, in a macabre scene immediately after, it is the corpses of deceitful Ananias and Saphira that fall to the ground at Peter's feet (5:10).

Philip the Evangelist

Like Stephen, Philip is one of the seven, a Hellenist selected by his own and appointed by the Twelve to help solve the problem of distributing fairly to the needy. Now he is initiating an evangelistic mission that begins, perhaps surprisingly, in Samaria. There, Luke notes, "the crowd with one accord listened eagerly to what was said by Philip, hearing and seeing the signs that he did" (8:6). This statement is noteworthy for at least two reasons. First, it is significant that someone other than the apostles will be the first to have a successful mission in Samaria, especially since Luke, alone among the four evangelists, made a point of mentioning the Samaritans' rejection of Jesus and the Twelve after it became clear that Jesus was setting his face towards Jerusalem. In that story, John and his brother James ask Jesus if he wants them to call down fire from heaven to consume the unrepentant Samaritans (Luke 9:54). James' and John's reaction echoes 2 Kings 1:9–12, where the prophet Elijah called down fire from heaven to consume two companies of soldiers sent to capture him. Only a few verses earlier in Luke's gospel, it was John who complained to Jesus about someone who was successfully casting out demons— something the apostles themselves were unable to do (Luke 9:40). Now, in Acts 8, the apostolic mission is finally making its way to Samaria, but it is not John or some other member of the apostles doing signs and wonders, but Philip, an outsider.

It is also worth noting the specific term used by Luke to describe the people's enthusiastic response to Philip, for he tells us that the Samaritans listen *homothudón*, translated here as "with one accord." This would hardly merit attention if not for the fact that the word appears to be quite important to Luke in Acts, while fairly rare elsewhere in the Bible. In the Greek translation of the Hebrew Scriptures, the word is found mainly in the later wisdom literature, most frequently in the Book of Job but also in lesser known books such as Judith, 1 Esdras and 3 Maccabees. The only New Testament occurrence of the word outside of Acts is in Romans 15:6, where Paul calls Jew and Greek members of the church alike to glorify God "with one voice (*homothudón*)." In Acts, however, Luke uses it no less than ten times, at very significant points in the story. In Acts 2:46, 4:24, and 5:12, for example, the same word is used to show the close ties of the Jerusalem believers after Pentecost, who worshiped and prayed together. In 7:57, Luke uses it to describe the mutual rage of those whom Stephen accuses of hypocrisy and who go on to stone him. Later the same word is used in terms of the unanimous decision of the Jerusalem leaders to select representatives to send to Gentiles converts 15:25. The final two occurrences of the word in Acts, in 18:12 and 19:29 parallel the attack on Stephen, as enemies of the gospel make united attacks on Paul and his companions. Thus, although rare elsewhere in the New Testament, *homothudón* is Luke's preferred word for denoting common purpose on the part of a group, whether a friendly or combative group. The use of the term with regard to Philip is thus similar to the earlier uses in Acts, when applied to the apostles and Jerusalem believers and their positive response to the gospel and their life together.

This is significant, as it shows that God is bringing about new life and new community in Christ outside of Jerusalem, indeed, in territory that previously was considered as enemy territory. Today, we celebrate Pentecost as a particular day in which God as Holy Spirit came to the apostles in Jerusalem, but here, through Philip's proclamation and mighty works, a new Pentecost is rushing in, as it will again in other places later in Acts. What the Jerusalem believers have already experienced, the Samaritan believers encounter as well, and this is only the beginning as the gospel begins its expansion; as Luke reports, "So there was great joy in that city" (8:8).

But Luke immediately offers a hard reality check, making clear that not all there are "good Samaritans." The story that follows is to the Samaritan mission what the unhappy tale of Ananias and Sapphira was to the Jerusalem mission. Even as that deceitful couple tried to hold back a portion of their money from the apostles, so Simon Magus of Samaria sees the miraculous things that accompany the gospel message and tries to buy the Spirit's gifts. Simon has been something of a wonder-worker himself prior to Philip's arrival, but now he finds himself caught up in the city's enthusiasm about this new message, even going forward to be baptized. Simon of Samaria's traditional designation, "Magus," comes from the Greek

Simon of Samaria's traditional designation, "Magus," comes from the Greek word for "conjurer" or "magician."

word for "conjurer" or "magician." At this point, Luke tells us that "when the apostles at Jerusalem heard that Samaria had accepted the word of God, they sent Peter and John to them" (8:14). In other words, Philip may have initiated the good work in Samaria, but it still needs to be confirmed by the home base, as it were. Given the apostles' previous setbacks in Samaria, it is hard not to smile at the irony of Peter and John being sent there to confirm the successful work of another worker who was not one of the Twelve.

Irony aside, Peter and John's arrival, with the resulting confrontation between Peter and Simon Magus, evokes the parallel with the Ananias and Sapphira tale. Both cases include Peter in a disciplinary role and both involve money. Once again, the way that people deal with their possessions reveals their true and deepest response to the gospel of Jesus, and whether they have been corrupted by love of money and control. Now we see a similar situation with Simon Magus. Here, though, there is no deceit but outright bribery; he offers the apostles money in return for a share in the Spirit's power that he sees go out from them whenever they lay hands on people (8:19). Even as Peter made Ananias face the severity of his sin—"You did not lie to us but to God"—now he likewise challenges Simon— "May your silver perish with you, because you thought you could obtain God's gift with money!" (8:20). The key difference between the stories is that while both Ananias and Sapphira are destroyed, Simon appears to repent, begging Peter to pray for him that he might escape death. We are left wondering about Simon's fate, as the story ends abruptly with Peter and John's return to Jerusalem.

Philip does not stay in Samaria either but, following an angelic prompting, travels south on the road from Jerusalem to Gaza through the Judean wilderness. Once more, we see that as the apostles continue to remain close to their base in Jerusalem, it will be others, like Philip, who take the gospel message to Judea and Samaria and "to the ends of the earth," including Ethiopia. The story of the Ethiopian eunuch's conversion and baptism by Philip on the road to Gaza is a fascinating prelude to the more famous account that follows of Paul's conversion on the road to Damascus. Together, these stories remind us today that mission and ministry occur when we are on the move, not sitting back as disinterested spectators. Even as Matthew's gospel makes explicit the call of Jesus to his followers to "go," not "sit" (Matt. 28:19), so here we find Philip following Christ's explicit commission at the very beginning of Acts, acting as a witness and ambassador to a fellow journeyer. The fact that this stranger is from Ethiopia is not insignificant, for it was viewed as a hostile land far removed from the faith of Israel. Psalm 68:31 speaks of the remarkable day when God would turn even the most stubborn hearts: "Let bronze be brought from Egypt; let Ethiopia hasten to stretch out its hands to God".

> Psalm 68:31 speaks of the remarkable day when God would turn even the most stubborn hearts: "Let bronze be brought from Egypt; let Ethiopia hasten to stretch out its hands to God."

For his part, Acts says that Philip encountered not just any Ethiopian, but a royal court official of considerable influence on his way home from Jerusalem, trying to understand a passage from the book of the prophet Isaiah. Philip's opening question—"Do you understand what you are reading?" (8:30)—is a low-key invitation to a conversation about God and Jesus and new life. The Ethiopian official's enthusiastic response ("Look, here is water! What is to prevent me from being baptized?") is Luke's reminder that there are people hungry for the good news. It should not surprise us, then, that as the eunuch came out of the water Philip has already gone, "snatched away by the Spirit" like the prophets of long ago, to preach and teach, eventually reaching Caesarea, where he would settle (8:40). It is there that we find him years later when Paul and his colleagues pass through the city. For now, however, Luke leaves the evangelist Philip and moves from the Gaza road to the Damascus road.

The Seven and the Seventy

It is clear that changes are afoot as the close-knit apostolic community begins to give way to something unfamiliar and much more far-reaching. And it all started with the introduction of the seven. Interestingly, however, this is not the first time that Luke has introduced a "numbered" group besides the twelve to do apostolic work. Unlike the other three evangelists, Luke's gospel alone includes the commissioning of a group of seventy workers separate from the twelve, an action that both follows the commissioning of the apostles and mirrors it. In both cases, Luke uses the identical term *apésteilen* ("apostle" or "sent one") to show that Jesus sent the respective groups out. Consider also the similarities between the specific instructions to the two groups, and how the charges to the seventy missionaries actually expand on what is said to the twelve:

Take nothing for your journey, no staff, nor bag, nor bread, nor money-not even an extra tunic (Luke 9:3).	Carry no purse, no bag, no sandals; and greet no one on the road (Acts 10:4).
Whatever house you enter, stay there and leave from there (Luke 9:4).	Whatever house you enter, first say, "Peace to this house!" And if anyone is there who shares in peace, your peace will rest on that person; but if not, it will return to you. Remain in the same house, eating and drinking whatever they provide, for the laborer deserves to be paid. Do not move about from house to house (Acts10:5–7).
Wherever they do not welcome you, as you are leaving that town shake the dust off your feet as a testimony against them (Luke 9:5).	But whenever you enter a town and they do not welcome you, go out into its streets and say, "Even the dust of your town that clings to our feet, we wipe off in protest against you" (Acts 10:10–12).

Consider also the rationale for selecting the second group. After Luke explicitly mentions that the seventy were sent out ahead of Jesus to the places where he himself intended to go, the rationale for more workers is given: "The harvest is plentiful, but the laborers are few" (Luke 10:2). In fact, that same verse continues with a charge to the seventy to pray that God will send out still more laborers since the need is so great. But there may also have been another reason for the additional workers. Luke depicts the return of the twelve from their mission complaining about their inability to feed the vast crowds listening to Jesus. In this familiar tale of the feeding of the five thousand, we find the apostles asking Jesus to send the hungry crowds away, to refuse a kind of table fellowship to the masses. Luke records a short and direct response from Jesus: "You give them something to eat" (9.13).

Similarly, in Acts the appointment of the seven occurs within the context of complaints about unequal distribution to the needy Hellenist widows. Furthermore, as Stephen stood before his accusers in Acts, Luke tells us his face was transformed into something like the "face (*prosōpon*) of an angel," not unlike the altered face of Jesus during his account of the Transfiguration (Luke 9:29). Doxa, or "glory," is the key theme in both. The difference is that while Peter, James, and John—the inner circle—saw Jesus standing with Elijah and Moses, Stephen saw Jesus standing (same Greek verb, *hestōta*) at God's right hand. The apostles' foretaste prefigured, as it were, Stephen's visual feast.

Perhaps more importantly, Luke notes that although the apostles have been granted power and authority over all demons and diseases, even after their inner circle witnessed the glory of Jesus transfigured they are still powerless when confronted with a demon-possessed young boy. When another unnamed worker does exorcise a demon in the name of Jesus and John complains that he is not one of their number, Jesus is quick to reply, "Do not stop him; whoever is not against you is for you" (9:50). So it could be argued that Luke's point is that there is more than enough work to go around, and that it is the twelve's failure to truly fulfill their apostolic charge that leads to the need for commissioning and sending out another group of workers.

It has often been noted that the story of the seventy appears to echo that of the seventy elders whom God empowered for prophetic ministry after Moses admitted his inability to carry the load of responsibility for the people of Israel by himself: "I will take some of the spirit that is on you and put it on them; and they shall bear the burden of the people along with you so that you will not bear it all by yourself" (Num. 11:16–17). This may well have been in Luke's mind while relating the story of the commissioning of the seventy. However, the tale also prepares the way for the calling of the seven in Acts 6, and the beginnings of a movement away from the familiar terrain of Jerusalem and ultimately toward "the ends of the earth." The twelve commissioned the seven to a specific task—that of assuring equal distribution to newcomers and outsiders. They then take the next logical step and begin distributing and "serving" the gospel message to those not already receiving the attention of the twelve. In other words, they begin moving away from Jerusalem, from the temple, and from the familiar to the unknown.

"In those days, the disciples began to increase in number." This increase brings new challenges. The commissioning of new leaders to meet those challenges will lead, in turn, to the transformation of the entire system. Change is on the horizon, and it will take still other believers in other locations to do what could not be done in Jerusalem. Soon the followers of Jesus will gain a new name and a radically expanded membership, as a minor Jewish sect becomes something altogether more.

CHAPTER 4

Apostolic Change

Everliving God, whose will it is that all should come to you through your Son Jesus Christ: Inspire our witness to him, that all may know the power of his forgiveness and the hope of his resurrection.

FOR THE MISSION OF THE CHURCH,
THE BOOK OF COMMON PRAYER

With Stephen's death, things changed both quickly and dramatically. Luke reports that a "severe persecution began against the church in Jerusalem," resulting in a mass exodus of believers to the countryside. The upside to this is that, like Philip the evangelist, they took with them the gospel message to all Judea and Samaria. The scenery and the players in Acts are changing, as Peter, who until now has served as the chief protagonist and spokesperson of the Jerusalem phase of the mission, begins to decrease, though not before one more crucial moment onstage. And Luke's hero, the man from Tarsus, has an experience with the risen Christ that would transform not only his life, but the history of the world.

A Dangerous Man

He would eventually become one of the most famous, and arguably misunderstood, individuals in all of human history. But when we find him at the opening of Acts 9, Saul of Tarsus is simply a very dangerous man—at least as far as the followers of Jesus are concerned. Indeed, Acts reports that Saul is "still breathing threats and murder

"The Way" was one of the earliest descriptors for the followers of Christ, even before the term "Christians" came into being. It is found several times in Acts, including 9:2; 18:25; 19:9; 19:23; 22:4; 24:22.

against the disciples of the Lord," and requesting official sanction from the Jewish leaders in Jerusalem to arrest members of the Way living in Damascus. "The Way" was one of the earliest descriptors for the followers of Christ, even before the term "Christians" came into being. It is found several times in Acts, including 9:2; 18:25; 19:9; 19:23; 22:4; 24:22. The story is so familiar that few readers ever ask why Saul was so intent on destroying this new sectarian movement. It is not enough to say that he was simply an obsessed, murderous individual, because this popular image of Saul really does not fit the facts.

We are told later in Acts that he had studied at the feet of Gamaliel, a leading rabbi noted for his wisdom. It was this same Gamaliel who, earlier in Acts, called for a moderate response on the part of the Jewish council toward the apostles, arguing that this new movement would probably die out on its own. But if it turns out to be of divine origin, he warned, "you may even be found fighting against God!" (5:39). It was under such an astute mentor that Saul studied, and he soon became a rising rabbinic scholar in his own right. He himself later told the believers in Galatia that he advanced in Judaism beyond many of his peers largely because of his zeal "for the traditions of my ancestors" (Gal. 1:14). So what is this impressive, up-and-coming rabbi doing persecuting the followers of Jesus, especially when his mentor seems to have followed a much more lenient course?

Like a good detective story, the answer just might be hiding in plain sight. Gamaliel had encountered apostles like Peter and John who, while they did indeed believe that Jesus of Nazareth was the messiah, still showed every sign of being faithful, observant Jews, honoring the customs and traditions of the Jewish law and the temple. Saul of Tarsus is facing a different kind of follower; he has heard with his own ears the witness against Stephen: "We have heard him say that this Jesus of Nazareth* will destroy this place and will change the customs that Moses handed on to us" (6:14). Saul isn't crazy. He simply sees what Peter and the others seemed to miss: that Jesus really did change everything. To Peter and the other evangelists, Jesus was the one who would one day restore the kingdom to Israel, so they had little reason to move beyond the precincts of the temple. To Stephen, on the other hand, Jesus had made the temple and all it represented irrelevant, breaking through the exclusive boundary between Hebrews and Hellenists, Jews and Gentiles. If this dividing line is erased, Saul realized, there will be nothing to protect Israel from gradual assimilation into the surrounding heathen culture and eventual disintegration. To Saul, therefore, the very existence of Israel is at stake. This made Stephen a dangerous man, Saul believed, and this Jesus whom he proclaimed infinitely more dangerous. In the face of extreme peril, extreme measures were called for, and so Saul of Tarsus, pupil of Gamaliel, teacher of the law, protector of Israel, set out for Damascus, only to face the very reality he dreaded most.

"Now as he was going along and approaching Damascus, suddenly a light from heaven flashed around him" (9:3). As is often the case in tales of divine encounters, a bright light blazed forth, so intense that Saul fell to the ground. And although his companions joined him in seeing the light, only Saul heard the voice that followed: "Saul, Saul, why do you persecute me?" The double use of the name both emphasizes the importance of the call and brings to mind other similar divine encounters. An obvious comparison here is with the Old Testament hero Samuel, the last judge of Israel who as a young boy, in an-oft heard passage from 1 Samuel 3, heard a voice, "Samuel, Samuel," but did not know the identity of the one calling him. Even so, in Acts 9, Saul hears the voice but does not know who is addressing him. "Who are you, Lord?" he asked, only to receive the one answer he did not want to hear: "I am Jesus, whom you are persecuting. But get up and enter the city, and you will be told what you are to do." As he would often remind both friends and opponents alike in later years, Saul's encounter with Jesus was no less real, no less authentic than Peter's or any other apostle's. He may not have walked with Jesus for three years as they did, but he met him on the Damascus road and was forever changed as a result. Blinded, Saul did what he was told, allowed himself to be led into the city, and waited for three days.

> An obvious comparison here is with the Old Testament hero Samuel, the last judge of Israel who as a young boy, in an-oft heard passage from 1 Samuel 3, heard a voice, "Samuel, Samuel," but did not know the identity of the one calling him.

47

The story of Saul is as much about the conversions of other believers as it is about his. Enter Ananias, a disciple with the same name but a very different heart from the conniving Ananias, husband of Sapphira, whose greed was his undoing. Again, Luke offers a story that mirrors, or rather previews, the more familiar account of Peter and Cornelius the centurion that follows soon after. God comes to Ananias in a vision and tells him to go and lay hands on Saul for healing and blessing. And Ananias balks, convinced that this is a very bad idea: "Lord, I have heard from many about this man, how much evil he has done to your saints in Jerusalem" (9:13). But God makes it clear that this is not a request, but a divine imperative. Saul, the former persecutor of the new faith, would become Paul, evangelist of Christ, bringing the new faith not simply to the Jews, but to the Gentiles as well.

Luke presents us with two great ironies here. The first is that Saul has been right all along. This belief in Jesus will eventually undermine the strict boundaries of Judaism and allow the Gentiles full inclusion into the community. This is what Peter himself will be shocked to learn in his encounter with Cornelius. This is what Saul saw as the great danger in Stephen; this is what he fought against. Now, ironically, Saul will become the instrument of this full inclusion, this breaking down of boundaries. Now Saul himself will be the "dangerous one." Ananias did as he was instructed. Saul's sight is restored and immediately, Luke tells us, he begins to preach this new faith in the synagogues. Those who listened were understandably incredulous, knowing who he was and what he had been doing before. He became such a powerful force that Jews who previously would likely have cheered his name now sought ways to kill him: "So he went in and out among them in Jerusalem, speaking boldly in the name of the Lord. He spoke and argued with the Hellenists; but they were attempting to kill him" (9:28–29). The tables truly had turned, and Saul has to be protected by his former enemies, who send him down to Tarsus.

The second irony is that, upon Saul's arrival in Jerusalem, the apostles did not want to have anything to do with him. They were still afraid of him. It took Barnabas the good steward, appearing now for the second time in Acts, to vouch for this convert and secure a (reluctant) seal of approval from the apostles.

With this we see that phase two of the missionary movement is beginning to wind down, as "the church throughout Judea, Galilee, and Samaria had peace and was built up." It was almost time to move into the final phase Jesus predicted, in which Saul/Paul would take the gospel to the ends of the earth and the Gentiles who lived there. But first, Peter has one more decisive time in the spotlight.

Peter and Cornelius

In the remaining section of Acts 9, we find Peter moving beyond Jerusalem's borders, visiting the believers in outlying areas and, like Jesus, healing the lame and raising the dead. Luke is clearly reminding readers of the importance of Peter to the early church. Earlier, when Philip's preaching resulted in conversions in Samaria, it was Peter and John who came to give the work their apostolic blessing, their seal of approval. Now, we see a similar thing happening, although this time in advance. In succeeding chapters, Luke will show the spread of the gospel to the Gentiles, but this is such a radical concept that it is crucial to show up front how the new movement is still connected to the Jerusalem community. This is why the Cornelius account is so important; indeed, it is repeated again when Peter makes a report to the Jerusalem Council in Acts 15, even as Paul later relates the story of his conversion not once, but twice, thereby pointing to its significance.

The Cornelius story is also noteworthy because it does mark a culmination, in many ways, of what Luke has been saying all throughout his two-volume work about the exemplary faith of the outsider. Cornelius is Luke's ultimate outsider, a Roman centurion. After all, it was an anonymous centurion who, at the cross, pronounced Jesus "an innocent man" (Luke 23:47). Cornelius, however, is not only called by name but also noted as being "a centurion of the Italian Cohort" (10:1). The Italian Cohort was so named because they were all native Romans, stationed in Caesarea, a seaport named for Caesar Augustus and home to the Roman governor of the region. Not only was Cornelius an important man, Luke also makes sure that we know he was also a devout one, a man who

> The Italian Cohort was so named because they were all native Romans, stationed in Caesarea, a seaport named for Caesar Augustus and home to the Roman governor of the region.

"feared God," gave alms generously and prayed constantly to God. In essence, he was the ideal prototype of what was to come.

However, no matter how devout this "God-fearer" was, he was still uncircumcised and thus still "unclean." As in the case with Ananias, God came to Peter in a vision while he was staying in nearby Joppa. Already hungry, Peter saw in the vision a divine feast prepared for him: a sheet is lowered from heaven filled with

> all kinds of four-footed creatures and reptiles and birds of the air. Then he heard a voice saying, "Get up, Peter; kill and eat." But Peter said, "By no means, Lord; for I have never eaten anything that is profane or unclean." The voice said to him again, a second time, "What God has made clean, you must not call profane." This happened three times, and the thing was suddenly taken up to heaven. (10:12–16)

The problem was that the animals he saw before him are all on the forbidden list for a faithful Jew. It was the ultimate non-kosher banquet to which he was invited. It must have seemed to Peter to be cruel on God's part to taunt a famished man with food he could not eat. "Never," Peter proudly proclaims, "I have never eaten anything that is profane or unclean." But God's immediate response sums up all that Jesus had tried again and again to teach the apostles in Luke's gospel: "What God has made clean, you must not call profane."

Peter's initial reluctance in this tale, like that of Ananias in the story of Saul's conversion, is reasonable. In fact it is not unlike the reluctance of the priest and Levite to help the half-dead stranger in the parable of the Good Samaritan in Luke 10. Indeed, Peter's evangelistic mission to Cornelius and his household echoes the Old Testament tale of Jonah reluctantly preaching to the pagan people of Ninevah. Like the Ninevites, Cornelius responds positively to the gospel message and, like the Ethiopian eunuch earlier in Acts, asks to be baptized, both himself and his household. A Pentecost experience follows, and Peter's traveling companions are incredulous: "The circumcised believers who had come with Peter were astounded that the gift of the Holy Spirit had been poured out even on the Gentiles" (10:45). Peter has learned his lesson, at least for now—later Paul's letter to the Galatians relates how Peter's old prejudices crop up again. But for the moment, here in Acts, Luke shows in the person of Peter the apostolic acceptance of the coming Gentile mission. It is an "Aha!" moment in the life of the followers of Christ, a turning point in the mission to the ends of the earth. For Peter, as for Ananias and Jonah, the initial reluctance is understandable, but, from the divine standpoint, unacceptable. For God, "never" is not a very helpful word.

It is not surprising, however, that Peter is harshly criticized when he returns to Jerusalem after his baptism of Cornelius and many other Gentiles. The almost verbatim report of his vision and its aftermath does silence his fellow believers, though even their acceptance of God's redeeming work among the Gentiles is guarded: "They praised God, saying, "Then God has given even to the Gentiles the repentance that leads to life" (11:18). Having said this, they went back to their own life in community, in which there was no Gentile to be found. For the moment, the "mother church" remained immune from the revolution that was beginning to take place elsewhere, but in the conversion of Cornelius the stage was set for eventual change of the system.

"New Wine in New Wineskins"

As the Cornelius story ends, we find words that clearly resonate with the harsh aftermath of Stephen's death: "That day a severe persecution began against the church in Jerusalem, and all except the apostles were scattered throughout the countryside of Judea and Samaria. . . . Now, those who were scattered went from place to place, proclaiming the word" (8:1–4). Now Luke picks up this thread again. He reports, "Now those who were scattered because of the persecution that took place over Stephen traveled as far as Phoenicia, Cyprus, and Antioch"—but then adds a crucial disclaimer, "and they spoke the word to no one except Jews" (11:19). In many ways, this disclaimer is what the section sandwiched between these verses has been all about, which is the resistance on the part of faithful but nearsighted believers to move beyond their comfort level. In the very next verse, however, Luke goes on to say that there were some "from Cyprus and Cyrene who, on coming to Antioch, spoke to the Hellenists also." In his gospel Luke had included the challenge of Jesus to put "new wine in new wineskins"; now, in Acts, Luke makes clear yet again that it is the *newcomers* who are open to new possibilities even as the insiders continue to offer at least partial resistance. If real, lasting change was going to happen, if there was to be any chance for the movement to grow beyond its Jewish sectarian roots, then a new home base was needed. That base is going to be established in Antioch.

Known as the "queen of the east," Antioch had been a key city in Syria since its origin in 301 BCE. A climatic battle that year made Seleucus Nicator master of the region, and he immediately founded the city that would bear the name of his father, Antiochus. Legends say that Seleucus chose the site when he noticed an eagle in flight and followed its path. In any case, Antioch was not a port city—it was located about fifteen miles from the sea—but to the successive empires that ruled over it, the city remained a prosperous, cosmopolitan center. By the time that the followers of Jesus came to it, Antioch was third only to Rome and Alexandria in its importance in the Roman Empire. From its earliest days, it had been a place where Jews were welcomed alongside Syrians, Greeks, and Romans. As a center for potential missionary work, it would be hard to imagine a better place than Antioch of Syria.

Luke notes that a great number of people had already become believers in Antioch, and as with Samaria, the leaders back in Jerusalem wanted to make contact. Instead of sending Peter or another apostle, however, this time they send Barnabas as their emissary. This is now the third time that the "son of encouragement" is mentioned in Acts, and we are told that what he saw upon his arrival gave him genuine joy. There was no hanging back with Barnabas: he immediately began teaching and challenging the believers in Antioch, for, as Luke makes a point of reminding readers, Barnabas truly was "a good man, full of the Holy Spirit and of faith" (11:24). What is interesting is what Barnabas did next. Rather than continuing in a leadership role on his own, he went down to Tarsus, where Saul was, and brought Saul back with him to spend the year in Antioch. Later in Acts 13, Luke references another Antioch, located

> A climatic battle that year made Seleucus Nicator master of the region, and he immediately founded the city that would bear the name of his father, Antiochus. Legends say that Seleucus chose the site when he noticed an eagle in flight and followed its path.

> Later in Acts 13, Luke references another Antioch, located not in Syria but rather in Pisidia. The fact is that Seleucus actually named several cities Antioch, as his father's name, Antiochus.

not in Syria but rather in Pisidia. The fact is that Seleucus actually named several cities Antioch, as his father's name, Antiochus. It was a move that showed equal parts perception and nurturing on the part of Barnabas, as he saw in Saul remarkable gifts for leadership and mentored him in the use of those gifts. Once again, Barnabas modeled exemplary stewardship, not of money but of people.

"So it was that for an entire year they associated with* the church and taught a great many people, and it was in Antioch that the disciples were first called 'Christians'" (11:26). Here we come to what may be one of the most understated verses of the New Testament, especially given the momentous news it reports. For although Pentecost had witnessed the conversion of three thousand souls, and although great preaching and miracles had occurred in Jerusalem, Luke now puts it on record that it was in Antioch, not Jerusalem, that the disciples were first called Christians. We may celebrate Pentecost as the "birthday of the church," but in truth it was a still a Jewish sectarian movement at that point. It might be more accurate to speak of Pentecost as the beginning of a gestation period that came to fruition with something truly new in Antioch, a movement that was no longer simply one more part of Judaism. This was a separate group altogether, where believers were willing to reach out to people beyond the normal synagogue membership. By going on to record that a severe world famine has been predicted, however, Luke also reminds readers that this new base in Antioch is still intimately connected to Jerusalem. This time though, interestingly, as a supportive patron. The community in Antioch sends financial relief via Barnabas and Saul back to the impoverished believers living in Jerusalem and the surrounding Judean area (11:29).

Acts *against* the Apostles

As Barnabas and Saul make their way to Jerusalem, Luke turns the spotlight one last time onto the twelve disciples, or more specifically, to two of the original apostles, James and Peter. The villain of the chapter is Herod Agrippa I, part of the so-called Herodian line. Agrippa was the grandson of Herod the Great, that famous ruler whose life and times are highlighted outside the New Testament by the Jewish historian Josephus, but whose biblical appearances are

Herod Agrippa also is to be distinguished from Herod Antipas, son of the Herod the Great, who had figured prominently in the death of John the Baptist and the trial of Jesus.

limited to the nativity narratives in Matthew and Luke. Herod Agrippa also is to be distinguished from Herod Antipas, son of the Herod the Great, who had figured prominently in the death of John the Baptist and the trial of Jesus. Educated with the future Emperor Claudius in Rome, Herod Agrippa was known as much for his cunning as for his ruthless ambition, allying himself with Caligula against the Emperor Tiberius. When Caligula himself became emperor, Herod Agrippa in turn prospered, and eventually under the imperial reign of his old friend Claudius, gained even greater power, overseeing Judea and Samaria. Shrewdly, he sided with those Jews opposing the newly differentiated Christian movement, and ordered the death of an apostle.

That the first member of the Twelve to be martyred was one of the inner circle is perhaps grimly appropriate. Along with his brother John and Simon Peter, James had been one of the first chosen by Jesus, a former Galilean fisherman turned evangelist, a "fisher of people." In the earliest chapters of Acts, it was John who was most often seen with Peter; now, in chapter 12, it is the other "son of thunder" (as the sons of Zebedee were known) who became the first apostle to die for his faith under the order of Herod Agrippa. Unfortunately, there is no grand speech at the moment of death for James, as we saw with Stephen. Rather, the apostle's death by the sword comes almost as a stark footnote in the account—"He had James, the brother of John, killed with the sword"—a preface to the much longer story of Peter's arrest and imprisonment.

Peter's tale follows the classic biblical formula of the faithful servant of God who is unjustly imprisoned and then freed by divine power, the most famous example perhaps being the three men in the furnace in the book of Daniel. In Peter's case, we see two familiar Lukan elements, prayer and angelic intervention. Against the backdrop of the community's "fervent prayers" for him, we hear the story of Peter's release. Chained and surrounded by guards, Peter feels a tap on his side and looks up to see an angel of the Lord, who tells him to rise and dress quickly. The chains fall off and the angel leads him out. The event is so surreal, Luke reports, that Peter at first thinks this is simply a vision, but eventually he finds himself safe outside the gate. He makes his way to the house of Mary, relative of Barnabas and mother of John, also called Mark, who has tradition-ally been associated with Mark's gospel, from which Luke, like Matthew, drew much material for his own. What happens then has the feel of slapstick comedy. The young servant girl at the door, Rhoda, recognizes Peter's voice but in her excitement left him at the gate as she ran back in to tell the still-praying group of believers. Again, like a predictable comedy routine, they do not believe Rhoda—"You are out of your mind!"—even though they have been praying fervently for Peter. Then they debate back and forth on whether it is Peter or his angel or none of the above . . . all the time while poor Peter is knocking outside, no doubt nervous about being caught and imprisoned all over again! Whatever Luke's reason for including such details, we find here that the drama of divine inter-vention is balanced with the foibles of fallible human beings. When they finally realize that it really is Peter at the gate, they open up and start in with a barrage of questions. Peter motions them to be silent and then tells his story, adding an intriguing postscript: "Tell this to James and to the believers" (12:17).

This is the first mention of James, known as "the brother of the Lord," who along with a group known as "the elders" began to appear and represent the next phase of leadership in Jerusalem, following that of Peter and the original apostles. A subtle shift was occurring in the church's life, and Luke notes it here first. Peter, instead of returning to his home base in Jerusalem, moves on to Caesarea, where once long ago he had first proclaimed Jesus as the Christ. The Jerusalem believers will now be led by James and the elders. The "mother church," which until now has seemed impervious to change, is itself changing.

In the prophecy of Isaiah to the exiled people of Israel we find God proclaiming, "I am about to do a new thing; now it springs forth, do you not perceive it?" (Isa. 43:19). The story of God's people is that they usually have not perceived God's new thing, or, if they did, they do not necessarily acknowledge that God is really the one who is behind it. In any age, change does not come easily, and this was certainly true for the first generation of believers. In Luke's gospel, just to give one example, Peter, James, and John had begged Jesus to let them hold onto the moment of transfiguration the high mountain, to preserve it in time forever (9:33). Now, at the close of Acts 12, James has been killed, John has disappeared from the scene, and Peter is no longer the key leader in Jerusalem. Like Peter, the Jerusalem church itself was beginning to wane in importance, though both apostle and apostolic base would have one more time in the spotlight. But now Antioch has become the base for a new set of missionary endeavors that would reach beyond boundaries both ethnic and geographic. And the apostles sent out from that base would be none other than those former neophytes, Barnabas and Saul. Soon, they would be "turning the world upside down."

For now, it is the world of the first believers that is being been turned upside down in ways they could not have imagined a short time before. As Luke's fast-paced account conveys, a lot changed in a very short time. From the shadow of the Jerusalem temple to Antioch and beyond, God was indeed doing a new thing through the power of the Spirit, just as Jesus had promised back at the very beginning. The next generation of believers—of Christians—is on the move, and all that they need is the acceptance of their mission from those first-generation apostles who are not necessarily comfortable with all the changes taking place.

What is needed is a compromise.

CHAPTER 5

Apostolic Compromise

*Grant O God, that following the example
of your servant James the Just, brother of
our Lord, your Church may give itself
continually to prayer and to the reconciliation of all who are at variance and enmity.*

COLLECT FOR THE FEAST OF JAMES THE JUST,
THE BOOK OF COMMON PRAYER

The Acts of the Apostles is still the title, but the "apostles" in question are about to change. Now Acts takes the step to which Luke has been pointing for several chapters. Antioch is the springboard from which Barnabas and Saul are about to dive into far deeper waters as their target audience expands and, ultimately, the full meaning of Jesus as Savior for all. But to do so would mean having the clear support of the "mother church" and that in turn would mean compromise. By the end of this section of Acts, Peter and the rest of the original apostles will disappear from view completely as a great partnership comes to an end, and the man from Tarsus will become forever known as Paul.

When the curtain opens in Acts 13, the setting is Antioch, where a small group of Christian leaders are about to appoint two of their own for a new phase of missionary movement. Luke names three specific persons besides Barnabas and Saul as "prophets and teachers" in the Anthochene church: Simeon, who was called Niger, Lucius of Cyrene, and Manaen, a member of the court of Herod the king. Nothing more is known of any of them, though there has been some conjecture about each one. Simeon (or Symeon, bearing both a Hebrew name and a Gentile designation) Niger is not mentioned again. Lucius was likely one of those "men from Cyprus and Cyrene" (11:20) who preached the good news to Hellenists. Some have even suggested that he is Luke himself, although that makes less sense; later in Acts Luke appears to include himself in the narrative through use of the first person plural, "we," but here speaks of Lucius in the third person. Manaen, with a Greek form of the Hebrew name "Menahem," meaning "consoler," is said to have grown up in some way with Herod "the tetrarch," Herod Antipas, son of Herod the Great. Although the three appear only here in Acts, what they do in their brief appearance will change the course of Christianity.

As with the selection of Matthias in the opening chapter of Acts, the decision-making here included a time of prayer and fasting. Unlike that earlier account, Luke makes it explicit this time that it was the Holy Spirit who is managing the outcome: "Set apart for me Barnabas and Saul for the work to which I have called them" (13:2). After further prayer and fasting, the Antioch leaders laid hands on them and "sent them off." The word here for "sent" is not the same as *apostel*, but it is a word with a rich scriptural heritage that speaks of those who are sent out for mission. Thus this brief section parallels the Jerusalem gathering, and Luke seems to insist that Barnabas and Saul are no less apostles of Antioch than Peter and the Twelve were apostles of Jerusalem. The chief difference is that Barnabas and Saul do not stay in Antioch, but go forth from there. Indeed, immediately after their appointment, these "sent ones" leave and go to Seleucia, from where they sail to Cyprus and arrive at Salamis. Almost as an afterthought, Luke mentions that they have brought John as a *hupā retās*, or "attendant," to assist them. This, of course, is John Mark, the cousin of Barnabas, and the brief reference to him here is significant for reasons that will be become clear later on.

Other examples of *hupāretās* in the New Testament are of a king's attendant (John 18:36), an officer of the Sanhedrin (Matt. 26:58), and a synagogue assistant (Luke 4:20).

Saul Becomes Paul

As with Peter's confrontation with Simon Magus, Luke introduces another so-called magician, Elymas by name, who opposes Barnabas and Saul by attempting to influence their host, Sergius Paulus, against the message they brought. It is at this point that Luke, in another wonderfully understated example, notes a moment of transition in the life of Saul, the life of the church, and the history of the world: "But Saul, also known as Paul, filled with the Holy Spirit, looked intently at him" (13:9). As in typical fashion for Luke, Saul/Paul is described as a person "filled with the Holy Spirit," thereby pointing to both the source and the coming direction of his ministry. The change in name is not, as with Simon Peter or Joseph Barnabas, the conferring of a new name, but literally a second name that he has always had. It speaks to the fact that Saul, now Paul, is by birth both "a member of the people of Israel, of the tribe of Benjamin, a Hebrew born of Hebrew" (Phil. 3:5), and "a Roman citizen" (Acts 22:28). Saul is his Hebrew name, named perhaps for the first king of Israel, who was also a member of the tribe of Benjamin. Paul, or Paulus, is his Roman name, representing a citizenship that he inherited at birth.

Paul's citizenship was the result either of honors bestowed upon his parents for service to the Empire or of being a resident of the influential city of Tarsus.

> Paul's citizenship was the result either of honors bestowed upon his parents for service to the Empire or of being a resident of the influential city of Tarsus.

On a practical level, the Roman name will later serve him well, but the chief importance is that it implicitly marks his final evolution from Gamaliel's former student and rabbi, Saul, to the apostle to the Gentiles known as Paul. As a preview of coming attractions, Paul strikes Elymas temporarily blind, just as he himself had once been, and then, Luke reports that "Paul and his companions set sail for Paphos and came to Perga in Pamphylia" (13:13). The former apprentice has truly come into his own. No longer would it be written, "Barnabas and Saul" but now "Paul and Barnabas" (13:42) or "Paul and his companions." Sadly, even as Luke notes the emergence of a leader in Paul, he also observes that John Mark, the cousin of Barnabas, has left the group and—perhaps significantly—returned to Jerusalem. Even as the new apostles began to move towards the ends of the earth, John took a step backwards to the familiar and the comfortable. Perhaps this is too harsh a critique, but the reality of John's departure, whatever his specific reasons, would have profound consequences later. Paul took notice of which companions really were willing to move forward in faith together and which were not. Paul has often been misunderstood as an arrogant loner in need of no one, but it is rather because he so highly valued his companions that he resented those who abandoned comrades, as he believed John Mark had done.

Hostility and Welcome

Before his conversion, Paul had worried about how the new faith would break down the barrier between faithful Jews and unclean Gentiles. Now he will learn that he was not the only one who recognized this threat, as he and Barnabas began their preaching mission in another Antioch, this one in the region of Pisidia in what was known as Lesser Asia. What will become a familiar formula in Paul's ministry begins here, as we find him going first to the synagogue, there facing first curiosity and then strong hostility. It began innocently enough, after the customary reading of the Torah and the Prophets, as the synagogue officials turned to Paul and Barnabas and invited them to share a "word of exhortation" (13:15). This moment is noticeably similar to that in Luke's gospel where Jesus was invited by the officials in his hometown synagogue to read from Isaiah and speak about it. As Paul begins his address here, it is possible to see the initial nods of approval from his listeners as he spoke of God choosing their ancestors and making them great in the land of Egypt. But as Paul moves forward in his capsule summary of Israel's history, he makes an unexpected leap as he comes to David—"Of this man's posterity God has brought to Israel a Savior, Jesus, as promised"—and goes on to describe the death of Jesus at the hands of those religious leaders and followers in Jerusalem who "did not recognize him or understand the words of the prophets." Paul concludes with an invitation and warning: "By this Jesus everyone who believes is set free from all those sins from which you could not be freed by the law of Moses" (13:23–39). Paul the Jewish rabbi has truly become Paul the Christian witness.

His audience was impressed, and after the synagogue meeting many asked Paul and Barnabas to continue the conversation, which they did the following Sabbath. This time, however, jealous Jewish leaders speak out against the two. They must have prevailed to some degree, because Paul and Barnabas' retort is equally sharp and unyielding, condemning those who reject their message as "unworthy of eternal life" and promising now to take that message to the Gentiles (13:46). The difference in response is predictable: while Gentiles are delighted to find that they can find a way to God that previously has been denied them, the Jewish leaders drive Paul and Barnabas out of the region.

As the pair make their way to another city, Iconium, the pattern repeats itself, so that "the residents of the city were divided; some sided with the Jews, and some with the apostles" (14:4). This is a significant verse, for Luke here actually refers to Paul and Barnabas as "apostles," a term previously reserved for the Twelve. Some scholars have tried to argue that this is an editorial error or misreading in an attempt to deal with the otherwise obvious statement that Luke is making. Even as Peter and the rest of the Twelve had been chosen apostles, sent to Jerusalem and ordered to continue on from there, so now it is Paul and Barnabas who have been sent out from Antioch of Syria by the Spirit to take the good news of Jesus Christ to the ends of the earth. As Antioch was the place where the believers were first called Christians, here we see Luke explicitly call Paul and Barnabas apostles precisely when they begin their ministry to the Gentiles. In his own letters to the new churches, against those who argued that such status was reserved only for the Twelve, Paul again and again will have to defend his apostleship. Just as Peter and the others devoted themselves to spreading the gospel to the Jewish people, he writes, so he and his companions have been called by God to carry the salvation message to the Gentiles. Here it is Luke who makes a similar argument, clearly showing that God is with Paul and Barnabas, sending them forth with apostolic authority and power.

"The Gods Have Come Down to Us!"

When Paul and Barnabas arrive in Lystra to continue their evangelistic work, Luke offers a new twist on what would otherwise be another familiar scene of healing. Paul, like Peter before him at the Beautiful Gate in Jerusalem, sees a crippled man and commands him to get up, which the man immediately does. At this point, something unexpected happens. The local people looking on are not religious Jews on their way to make their temple sacrifices, such as Peter had faced, but rather polytheistic Gentiles who see in this miracle evidence that the gods they worship have come down in human form. As Luke presents it, "Barnabas they called Zeus, and Paul they called Hermes, because he was the chief speaker" (14:12). The priest of Zeus even prepares to make sacrifices to them! Barnabas and Paul are horrified; Luke notes that they tear their clothes, a sign of deep emotion in the face of blasphemy or death. Proceeding to rush into the crowd, they implore these Gentiles to cease their misplaced worship: "Friends,* why are you doing this? We are mortals just like you, and we bring you good news, that you should turn from these worthless things to the living God" (14:15). It is interesting that here Paul sees for the first time that he will face a different challenge in preaching to the Gentiles than he did when addressing a Jewish audience. No longer could he quote the scriptures and expect his listeners to understand; even the rabbinic mode of discourse with which he was most comfortable will now be less useful, as he faces a different kind of people who have not been brought up in the faith of Israel, worshiping one God. He learned something else that day, for the Jews from Antioch of Pisidia and Iconium made their way to the scene and won over the crowds, so that they in turn "stoned Paul and dragged him out of the city, supposing that he was dead" (14:19). Paul thus learned, as Jesus did fairly quickly, that people are infinitely fickle.

One thing that is particularly interesting in Paul's response to the Gentiles who wanted to worship Barnabas and him as gods is how he explained the gospel to them without being able to use the Hebrew scriptures. His audience would not have understood or appreciated such efforts, in any case. Instead, Paul spoke to them of God as nature's creator, telling them that nature itself is the true "witness" of God's goodness, "giving you rains from heaven and fruitful seasons, and filling you with food and your hearts with joy" (14:17). This strategy will be expanded in his famous sermon at the

Athenian Areopagus in Acts 17, and it showed a new way to sharing the gospel to a people with no prior religious training in the Judaism with which he himself had been raised.

Acts 14 concludes with a travelogue of Paul's and Barnabas' return through the places they have visited on this first apostolic journey, going back through Lystra, Iconium, and Antioch, and reminding their fellow disciples in those places that it is "through many persecutions that we must enter the kingdom of God" (14:22).

In a rare piece of explicit correlation between Acts and one of the letters, 2 Timothy 3:11 also speaks of "the persecution and suffering that happened to me in Anitoch, Iconium, and Lystra."

The pair do more than simply preach again in these places. With prayer and fasting, they also appointed *presbuteroi*, or "elders," in each Christian community. This is something new for the church. As we come to Acts 15, we will find that there are elders already in place in Jerusalem under the leadership of James, the brother of Jesus, but Luke does not mention how Jerusalem's management moved from Peter and the apostles to James and the elders. Here, however, we see Paul and Barnabas directly involved in selecting and appointing elders to oversee the communities that the apostles have founded. It is noteworthy that these second-generation leaders are not themselves called "apostles," for they were not sent off from those communities but rather called to stay and nurture the new churches. The apostles' role involves proclamation and initiation, while the presbyters are to focus on ongoing encouragement and cultivation. In the kind of agricultural metaphor that Jesus used often, and Paul takes up in 1 Corinthians, Paul and Barnabas sowed the seeds, and the elders they put in place watered the seeds so that they could grow.

The specific term Luke uses to describe these elders, *presbuteroi*, is interesting. Until this point, he has spoken of *apostoloi* and, with Stephen and the Seven, *diakonoi*. This new designation of presbyter or elder speaks of an office that has some direct resonances with Judaism, for the *presbuteroi* were members of the Sanhedrin, the great council that oversaw the religious life of Israel. In Israel's earlier days, the judges were often those of more mature years and experience, and were stationary—they were not itinerant preachers, but teachers who stayed in one place to train those under their charge. Even so, Paul and Barnabas differentiated between their role as evangelists and church planters as opposed to those who would then take those churches and strengthen them, build them up, and nurture the members within. Neither Paul in his letters nor Luke in his narrative ever refer to Christian synagogues, but the instructions given to those who oversaw these faith communities (or *ekklesia*) are similar to those given to synagogue leaders.

Having left the churches they planted in good hands, Paul and Barnabas make their way back to Antioch, bringing themselves full circle to "where they had been commended to the grace of God for the work that they had completed" (14:26). The report they give focused on how God has "opened a door of faith" for the Gentiles, a message that would reach beyond Antioch and trigger some anxious reactions.

The First Jerusalem Council

The opposition that Paul and Barnabas first faced in their missionary work is far from over. That opposition will now take a different form, less violent but no less virulent, as Paul and his Judaizer opponents make their way to Jerusalem for what would become known as the First Council of the Church. These "Judaizers" taught the Gentile Christians whom Paul and Barnabas had reached that they could not truly be saved unless they went further and were circumcised, thereby becoming faithful, Torah-adherent Jews. This will be the first time the new church has to face such attitudes, but certainly not the last. Throughout the centuries since then, there have always been some who have argued that something more is needed beyond God's grace and our response of faith. For Paul, who earlier had dreaded this very thing, if Christ really is to be understood as Savior, then he is Savior of all, and to insist on further requirements for salvation is not only wrong-headed but erroneous. Paul and Barnabas therefore decide to take their case to the apostles and elders in Jerusalem. Along the way, much like politicians stumping for their cause, they told every believer they could find about the

These "Judaizers" taught the Gentile Christians whom Paul and Barnabas had reached that they could not truly be saved unless they went further and were circumcised, thereby becoming faithful, Torah-adherent Jews.

ways they saw the Holy Spirit at work among the Gentiles. They were well received by the members of the Jerusalem church when they first arrived, but quickly face opponents who belong to "the sect of the Pharisees" and demand that the Gentile converts "be circumcised and ordered to keep the law of Moses" (15:5). Luke notes that the apostles and elders debate the situation at length until Peter himself stands up and addresses the gathering.

Peter's appearance in this council will be his last in the book of Acts, but here he is fulfilling a crucial role. It is that of the denier-turned-witness, the one who knows personally what the grace of God can do. He also is the one who saw that grace at work in the household of Cornelius, the Roman centurion. Peter, who had exhibited strong initial resistance to the inclusion of Gentiles, was himself convinced in a vision from God that "in cleansing their hearts by faith, [God] made no distinction" between Jew and Gentile (15:9). Now he challenges his fellow leaders in Jerusalem not to burden the new converts with "a yoke that neither our ancestors nor we have been able to bear" (15:10). It is Peter's final speech in Acts, and quite possibly his finest moment.

Peter is followed by Paul and Barnabas, who speak of the signs and wonders they have seen God accomplish among the Gentiles. The whole gathering listens with rapt attention. Finally, after all has been reported, James, the leader of the Jerusalem church, speaks up. It is worth recalling that this James is to be distinguished from the two apostles who bore the same name, both the now-martyred son of Zebedee and the so-called James the Less. Known by his designation "the Just," this James is traditionally understood as the "brother of the Lord." James appears by name as one of the brothers of Jesus in both Mark 6:3 and Matthew 13:55, along with Joses, Judas, and Simon as well as unnamed and unnumbered sisters. It is interesting that in his response to Peter's speech James calls Peter "Simeon," his Aramaic name, and not the Greek, Petros. This is a blunt reminder that those to whom James is about to appeal are Jewish Christians. He continues by immediately quoting the Hebrew Scriptures, thereby appealing to the sacred text instead of to

> James appears by name as one of the brothers of Jesus in both Mark 6:3 and Matthew 13:55, along with Joses, Judas, and Simon as well as unnamed and unnumbered sisters.

personal experience of the Holy Spirit's work among the Gentiles, as Paul and Barnabas—and even Peter—did.

James thus leads the way to a decision that could rightly be called "the great compromise," for it has something that appealed to both sides while, in the end, stopping short of either side's full desire. On the one hand, James recommends that the leadership in Jerusalem "not trouble those Gentiles who are turning to God" (15:19), meaning not force them to be circumcised as the Judaizers demanded. On the other hand, he also suggests that the Gentiles be clearly instructed to abstain from those things that were most obviously odious to faithful Jews, including food that has been sacrificed to idols, sexual acts associated with pagan ways, or dietary items most strenuously condemned by the Torah. This is not a random list. Rather, it means that the Jerusalem leaders can, in essence, maintain some control over the ever-dreaded threat of intermingling. For what has preserved Hebrew identity and culture for so long is the "set-apartness" of the Jewish people from those people and practices deemed unclean. To take seriously the restrictions James is proposing would mean serious disengagement on the part of Gentile believers from their familiar relational networks. In other words, they could remain uncircumcised as long as they lived as if they were.

The compromise was accepted by the gathering and together they decide to send the message to the church in Antioch via Paul and Barnabas, along with two other Jerusalem leaders, Judas, called Barsabbas, and Silas, the latter of whom will later become an important companion of Paul's. The decision to send these two Jerusalem insiders with Paul and Barnabas is interesting, and shows how much the role of Barnabas has changed vis-à-vis the apostles. Earlier, he was the one who had been able to vouch for Paul, and the one whom the apostles felt comfortable sending to Antioch to check on the evangelistic activity there. Now, Barnabas and Paul together are clearly associated with Antioch, and so it becomes important for others more obviously connected with Jerusalem to accompany them and to carry the message from the apostles and elders to "the believers of Gentile origin in Antioch, Syria, and Cilicia" (15:23).

The letter they brought with them, and the oral report that accompanied it, offered both reassurance and recommendation. The

Gentile believers would not have to be circumcised, but they would need to refrain from "what has been sacrificed to idols and from blood and from what is strangled and from fornication" (15:29). The Gentiles welcome the message and are encouraged by the words of Judas and Silas, who eventually make their way back to Jerusalem while Paul and Barnabas remain in Antioch, teaching and preaching. It is a significant moment, providing confirmation that the Gentiles have indeed been accepted into a new faith and not simply a sect of Judaism. Yet the solution was far from perfect, as Paul would make clear years later in his letter to the Christians in Galatia. There, in the second chapter, he speaks at length about opposing Peter to his face in Antioch when the apostle, after showing no qualms about being at the table with Gentile Christians, suddenly withdrew and refused to eat with them when representatives from James and the Jerusalem leadership came into town. For until certain people came from James, he used to eat with the Gentiles. But after they came, he drew back and kept himself separate for fear of the circumcision faction. And the other Jews joined him in this hypocrisy, so that even Barnabas was led astray by their hypocrisy (Gal. 2:12–13). Apparently the Gentiles' acceptance of the Jerusalem Council's recommendations could not overturn years—even centuries—of deeply ingrained prejudices and fears. The solution was far from perfect, but it was a huge step forward, a glimpse into the reality that would slowly evolve as the church began to recognize what Paul would later assert, "a person is justified not by the works of the law but through faith in Jesus Christ" (Gal. 2:16).

> For until certain people came from James, he used to eat with the Gentiles. But after they came, he drew back and kept himself separate for fear of the circumcision faction. And the other Jews joined him in this hypocrisy, so that even Barnabas was led astray by their hypocrisy. (Gal. 2:12–13)

The End of a Partnership

It began innocently enough. Paul suggested to Barnabas that they return to the faith communities they had established in order to see how they were faring. Barnabas suggested in turn that they take his cousin John Mark with them. This is when the fireworks began. Paul did not want to take along someone who he viewed as a deserter. For John Mark had accompanied the pair in their earliest missionary work, only to leave them when things became difficult in Pamphylia. Luke never shares exactly why John Mark deserted them, but what is clear is that Barnabas wanted to give his cousin a second chance and Paul absolutely did not. It has been suggested that John Mark might have disagreed with Paul's strong position about Gentile inclusion or perhaps he was simply scared by the violent opposition they faced.

> It has been suggested that John Mark might have disagreed with Paul's strong position about Gentile inclusion or perhaps he was simply scared by the violent opposition they faced.

Their positions on this issue are consistent with their respective characters and values. From the moment he first appeared, Barnabas was recognized as an encourager, a bridge-builder, a nurturer. If not for him, Paul would not even have been accepted by the apostles. Thus it is not at all surprising that Barnabas would insist that John Mark be allowed to join their party once more. Likewise, from the start Paul understood the Christian gospel to be about full inclusion. If Jesus is savior, he is savior of all. Whether John Mark left because of fear or a difference of opinion, Paul saw him as a liability in the crucial work of bringing the good news of salvation through Jesus to the Gentiles. The gospel work was too important and there were too many souls at stake to risk letting a deserter rejoin their company, only to have him possibly abandon them once again. Luke reports the unhappy news that "the disagreement became so sharp that they parted company" (15:39). Here we find another example of Luke's understatement, for the tragedy here is that two partners who had endured so much together now find that their different convictions take them in opposite directions. The silver lining in this situation is that they both continued the apostolic work, Barnabas with John Mark by his side, and Paul taking Silas, the first of several new missionary companions. It was the end of an era, but certainly not the end of the story.

CHAPTER 6

Apostolic Colleagues

*Grant that by the prayers and labors of
your holy Church, all the nations of the
earth may be brought to know and worship
you as you have been revealed by your Son.*

COLLECT FOR THE MISSION OF THE CHURCH, THE
BOOK OF COMMON PRAYER

Silas was the first of Paul's companions after he separated
from Barnabas, but he certainly would not be the last.
Despite the popular notion that Paul was an irascible "lone
wolf," again and again he makes it clear in his letters that
he does not work alone, but always as part of a team. The
salutation that begins each letter almost always reads, "Paul
and _____, to the church in. . . ." Likewise, at the
close of each letter Paul includes a long list of friends and
co-workers who either send their greetings along with
Paul's or are on the receiving end of his greetings. For Paul,
apostolic ministry was not a solo effort. In Acts, Luke
depicts the apostle as a leader who models community life
in his own vocational partnerships. Silas, Timothy, Titus
(though not mentioned by name in Acts), Lydia, Phoebe,
Priscilla and Aquila, and Luke himself are among those
who will join Paul in his apostolic work, and through
whom the world will be turned upside down.

Honoring God

The split with Barnabas, disappointing as it was, does not
slow Paul down. Instead, the apostle recruits Silas to join

him as he makes his way to Derbe and Lystra, where he quickly finds another teammate, a young soon-to-be-apprentice named Timothy. "Timothy" literally means "honoring God," and by all indications the designation was an appropriate one. Born of a Jewish Christian mother named Eunice and an unbelieving Greek father, Timothy was apparently not raised in the Jewish faith, as he was not even circumcised in infancy. His faith, though, was genuine, due in large part to the examples he had in his mother and in his grandmother: "I am reminded of your sincere faith, a faith that lived first in your grandmother Lois and your mother Eunice and now, I am sure, lives in you" (2 Tim. 1:5). It may well be that during Paul's first missionary journey to Derbe and Lystra, Eunice and Lois embraced the good news and became Christians. Certainly this appears to be the case with Timothy himself, who knows about the struggles and persecutions Paul had encountered for the sake of Christ on that earlier journey. Timothy will go on to become one of the most famous of Paul's companions; his name appears as Paul's co-worker in the salutations of several of the letters (1 and 2 Thessalonians, 2 Corinthians, Philippians, Colossians, and Philemon), and two of the epistles in the New Testament are actually named for him. Before he can even begin to work with the apostle, however, there is one major obstacle to overcome.

> "Timothy" literally means "honoring God," and by all indications the designation was an appropriate one.

Timothy had not been circumcised as an infant despite the fact that his mother was a Jew. Perhaps his father had intervened and denied the rite to his son. In any case, as we saw just recently in Acts, it was seen as a major concession on the part of Jewish Christians to allow Gentiles to come to Christ without being circumcised and therefore first becoming Jews. But here is an uncircumcised Jew, an altogether different case. Does the Torah now mean nothing to Paul? Is this neophyte Christian movement trying to antagonize faithful Jews? Timothy's inclusion not only as a believer but as a member of Paul's evangelistic team means that a concession on Paul's part is needed—or, more accurately, a concession on the part of Timothy. He was circumcised before going forth with Paul, something that will not be required later of Titus, who is entirely of Gentile origin (Gal. 2:3–5). The twin principles for Paul would be freedom in Christ and at the same time service to all. He therefore works with the same principle that the Jerusalem Council used: do not put up any unnecessary barriers to another person coming to Christ. If someone is a Gentile, then that person should not feel the need to become a Jew first. At the same time, if one is already Jewish, then that tradition should be honored. For Paul, in Christ there are no longer to be distinctions between "Jew or Greek" (Gal. 3:28), but he and his colleagues will still have to bend to expediency in helping people come to be in Christ.

On the Move

Paul and his companions are on the move, and Asia is their target area. Something, however, keeps preventing them from going there. They travel throughout Phrygia and Galatia, and across from Mysia, but are frustrated each time they attempt to move further east. No one could accuse these missionaries of giving up too easily, for each time they hit a wall, they move on to another potential gateway, determined to bring the gospel to Asia. Luke makes it clear, however, that it is the Holy Spirit, the Spirit of Jesus, who will not allow them to go into Asia. Paul finally gets the message when he has a night vision in which a European, "a man of Macedonia," begs Paul to "come and help us" (16:9). He does not have to ask twice, for Luke notes that Paul "immediately tried to cross over to Macedonia, convinced that God had called us to proclaim the good news to them" (16:10).

This last verse is an especially intriguing one, for it marks the beginning of what has been called the "we" section of Acts, referring to the change from third person to first person plural: "God had called *us* to proclaim the good news to them." "We" and "us" takes the place of "they" and "them," suggesting that the author of Acts, whom we call Luke, is now part of Paul's company. When he joined is not clear, but it is evident that the apostolic journey will no longer be simply a second-hand tale, but a personal account to be shared. This verse is also noteworthy because in the shift towards the western part of the empire, the Gentiles whom the apostolic team would encounter will be Roman instead of Greek. From the Jewish standpoint, this must have been an even more bitter pill to swallow, as the

Romans are the invaders, the abominable ones who have overrun and subjugated Palestine. These are Gentiles of a different sort, and so it must have been all the more important for Paul to reassure any fellow Jews who wondered about his motives and loyalty to God's chosen people.

In any case, Luke reports that "we set sail from Troas" and the group make its way ultimately to Philippi, a leading Roman settlement nestled in an agriculturally fertile plain, sheltered by mountains and connected by roadway to a nearby Aegean seaport named Neapolis. Named for Philip II of Macedon, father of Alexander the Great, Philippi first came into Roman hands after the battle of Pydna in 168 BCE, but arguably its most famous moment came in the year 42, as Octavian (later the Emperor Augustus) and Antony waged battle against the forces of Brutus and Cassius, that duo who earlier had been instrumental in the assassination of Julius Caesar. In the end, Octavian and Antony proved victorious, and Philippi was made a Roman colony. Eleven years later, after the battle of Actium, Philippi was reinforced and received the coveted *ius Italicum,* the honor that brought with it many privileges, especially immunity from taxation. In Paul's time Philippi was a Roman city of considerable importance and prestige because of its gold mines.

> In Paul's time Philippi was a Roman city of considerable importance and prestige because of its gold mines.

It is at Philippi that the apostle and his colleagues meet Lydia, a Greek proselyte from Thyatira in Asia Minor. Luke describes her as a "dealer in purple cloth" (16:14), an appropriate occupation—and a profitable one—given the fact that her native town was renowned for the manufacture of dyed woolen fabrics. Her name was not uncommon, linked with the important country of the same name to the west of Phrygia in Asia Minor. Lydia was a Jewish convert, a "God worshipper," who apparently gathered regularly with others at a place of prayer by the riverside. On this particular occasion she hears Paul preach for the first time and her heart opens to the message he proclaims. Her response is to be baptized, along with her household, and then to offer the hospitably of her home to Paul and his companions. It is likely that Lydia's home eventually became the center for the church in Philippi.

Prison

Being a colleague of Paul's could be hazardous duty. Barnabas learned that in Lystra, and now Silas is finding out for himself that apostolic work can land a person in jail. Luke begins the story with another "we" passage: "One day, as we were going to the place of prayer, we met a slave-girl who had a spirit of divination and brought her owners a great deal of money by fortune-telling" (16:16). The young woman follows Paul and the others, crying out and exclaiming about them for days on end. Finally, Paul has heard enough. The King James version of the New Testament says that the apostle is "grieved," but the original Greek is more accurately translated as "irritated" or "annoyed." (The same term is found earlier in Acts 4:2, when the Jewish authorities in Jerusalem were described as being "annoyed" by the disturbance being created by the Twelve). He commands the demon in the name of Jesus Christ to leave her, and "it came out that very hour." But the owners of the young woman, now restored to herself, are angry about losing their income-producer, so they take hold not only of Paul but Silas as well and bring them before the local authorities.

The charges against Paul and Silas are particularly interesting since they are the opposite of what formerly was said against the Christians. The charge is that Paul and Silas, as Jews, are "advocating customs that are not lawful for us as Romans to adopt or observe" (16:21). The Jerusalem Council had already addressed the fear of Gentile practices threatening the Jewish ways; here, the magistrates in Philippi are being warned against undue Jewish influence in this Roman city. Stripped, beaten, flogged, Paul and Silas are finally thrown into prison and held in a high security area with their feet chained.

There was little to celebrate, and yet this is exactly what Paul and Silas chose to do, praying and singing to God as their fellow prisoners listen in wonder. Next, in a parallel scene to Peter's miraculous release from prison in Acts 12, an earthquake knocks the prison doors wide open. The awakened jailer sees the open doors and obviously assumes that all the prisoners have escaped on his watch while he was dozing. Drawing his sword, he prepares to kill himself—only to hear Paul call out to him and reassure him that no one has left. All are still present. For the poor jailer, this must have seemed as miraculous as the earthquake itself. In a moment that, like other incidents in Acts, is almost cinematic in character, the Philippian jailer brings Paul and Silas out of the jail and asks, "Sirs, what must I do to be saved?" Their response is equally powerful and altogether simple: "Believe on the Lord Jesus, and you will be saved, you and your household" (16:30–31). They preach the good news as the whole household listens. After the jailer has washed Paul's and Silas' wounds, they in turn wash him and his household in the waters of baptism. Together they share a common meal, no longer jailer and prisoners, but fellow believers in Christ. As an epilogue to the tale, when the jailer brings news that the authorities are releasing Paul and Silas from prison, Paul actually demands an apology as a Roman citizen unjustly beaten and imprisoned. Because of his Roman citizenship, Paul does receive that apology, and he and his colleagues return to Lydia's.

Turning the World Upside Down

As Paul's story progresses in Acts, the names of the cities and regions mentioned in Luke's account begin to sound more familiar. Having already mentioned Galatia and Philippi, Luke now moves into the adventures of Paul and Silas in Thessalonica, Corinth, and Ephesus, as well as in Athens. It should be noted that Luke's story also remains in the third person plural throughout this section, which suggests that he was not with the duo during this period following their Philippian prison experience. As they come into Thessalonica, they are entering one of the chief towns of Macedonia, originally known as Therma but enlarged and renamed around 315 BCE by Cassander of Macedon after his wife, daughter of Philip II and step-sister of Alexander the Great. When the Romans conquered the region, Thessalonica was made the capital first of one of the four newly designated districts and later of the single Roman province of Macedonia. In the eventual final days of the Republic, the city took the side of Octavian and Antony and, like Philippi, was rewarded for its loyalty as it was named a "free city." By Paul's time, Thessalonica

By Paul's time, Thessalonica was a wealthy port city with a large population of Romans, Greeks and Jews. It was also a major stopping-point on the Via Egnatia, a major highway that ran from the Adriatic to the Hellespont.

was a wealthy port city with a large population of Romans, Greeks, and Jews. It was also a major stopping point on the Via Egnatia, a major highway that ran from the Adriatic to the Hellespont.

For Paul and Silas the first stop in the city is the synagogue, where they attempt to persuade members there that Jesus is the Messiah so many first-century Jews have been awaiting. Some are indeed convinced and join them, as did "many devout Greeks and not a few of the leading women" (17:4). Once again, it is not Paul's teaching about Jesus as much as his egalitarian openness to the inclusion of Gentiles and of women that result in enraged outbursts from some Jews. They even attack the home of Jason, where Paul and Silas are apparently lodging. (We know nothing more about Jason, who may or may not be the same person listed by Paul as a kinsman and fellow worker in Romans 16:21.) In any case, Luke notes that Jason and some other believers were dragged before the municipal authorities as the mob leaders shout out an unintentionally prophetic charge against Paul and his colleagues: "These people who have been turning the world upside down have come here also . . . . saying that there is another king named Jesus" (17:6–7). As with Jesus himself, the Christian missionaries are accused of treason against the emperor. After some kind of bail was received from Jason, Paul and Silas leave Thessalonica that very night.

Now they make their way further west to a city at the foot of Mount Bermius named Beroea, one of the most populated cities in Macedonia. Here they find much greater receptivity in the synagogue for their message, and here also they include and welcome Gentiles, both women and men. All might have gone well if not for the arrival of their Thessalonian opponents, who follow them to the new city and incite the crowds in Beroea against them. Once again, for his own safety, the believers send Paul away—but this time alone, as Silas and Timothy stay behind for a time until they catch up to him in Athens.

In the first century Athens was famous as a hub of learning and philosophy. Named for the goddess Athena, whom legends purported to have founded the city, this capital of Attica had a fascinating history and by the fifth century BCE was the center of of Greek culture. It was the backdrop for countless military and political dramas, including the Peloponnesian War, which ended in 404 BCE with Sparta's victory over the city. Less than a century later, Athens was on the losing side again when it joined Thebes' unsuccessful resistance against Philip of Macedon, and after Philip's murder came under the authority of his son, Alexander the Great. So great, however, was the fame of Athens that when Rome eventually came to rule over Greece, it was allowed some local autonomy and soon became the chief university town of the empire. It was a city of around 250,000 inhabitants when Paul first walked through its gateway.

As he entered Athens by way of the so-called "new road," Paul would have noticed the altar to an "unknown god" before making his way past the burial ground to the marketplace, the Agora, just north of the 200-foot high Acropolis in the center of the city. Surrounding him on every side were temples and statues to many gods and goddesses. It was popularly said among the philosophers that there were twice as many idols in Athens than in all the rest of Greece, and Luke remarks that Paul was *paroxun* or "distressed" (17:16) by what he witnessed. While the literal meaning of the word was "to sharpen," from the fifth century onward it was used metaphorically to convey a strong emotional response, and could be best conveyed, "to provoke," "to spur on," "to exasperate," "to rouse to anger." So what does Paul do? He goes immediately to the synagogue and the marketplace to spread his message.

It is interesting to note who is listening to Paul in the marketplace. No longer is he facing irate Jewish leaders who fear that his inclusive faith would break down completely the crucial boundaries between God's chosen people and those around them. No, in Athens the apostle instead faced philosophers, Epicureans and Stoics. The former group followed the teachings of Epicurus, a philosopher who lived in the late-third to second-century BC and made Athens his home base. With the decline of the classical Greek city-states and the loss of a sense of security, many were attracted to the very practical and life-affirming belief system Epicurus promoted. The oft-used description of his philosophy as "egoistic hedonism" can be misleading, for to Epicurus the pursuit of happiness is to be focused far more on the desires of the mind than on the urges of the body. Pain is the great evil, while pleasure is understood as the absence of pain, physical or mental. Absent from his philosophy, however, are any notions of a spiritual realm or life after death or the workings of Providence. The chief concern for Epicurus and his followers was the here and now, his ultimate goal a peace of mind that could transcend all circumstances.

The Stoics took their name from the "Painted Porch" in Athens, the "Stoa Poikile," where Zeno founded a school of philosophers that would eventually include such notables as Seneca and Marcus Aurelius, and had considerable influence in cities like Paul's native Tarsus. Simply put, the Stoics' chief principle, "Follow Nature," encourages harmony with and submission to the rational order of the universe, complete mastery of all emotions, and recognition of the importance of reason and humane conduct by individuals and by society as a whole. The Roman empire adapted much of the Stoic sense of orderliness in its own system of jurisprudence. Stoics balanced their belief that all the world is in some sense God, with divinity flowing through each part, while rejecting the more popular and, to them, uneducated religions of their time. The crucial issue for Stoics is not knowledge or worship in and of themselves, but how "following nature" could lead to an ethical, calm, and peaceful life of self-control and moral fortitude. Thus they bravely endured struggles and tribulations, confident that ultimately all things would work together for good if they remained true to the laws of nature, or providence.

These two philosophies of Epicurus and Zeno had several elements in common, despite some crucial distinctions. Some congruence can also be seen with the Christian faith that Paul and his colleagues are coming to proclaim. As the respective philosophers hear him speak in Athens, some consider the apostle to be a mere "babbler" and empty talker, but others are intrigued with both the similarities between what he is saying and what they themselves believe, and the obvious differences, which mostly involve Jesus. So they invite him to explain "this new teaching" he has brought with him, and to do so at the Areopagus (17:19). Also known as Mars Hill, the rocky height was named for Ares, the god of war, or Mars as he was called in the Roman pantheon. Judgment of capital offenses was held here, but also discussions of religious topics when a larger audience was desired. To the Areopagus, to Mars Hill, Paul goes. There he presents the same gospel message, but using very different arguments, that he earlier taught to his fellow Jews in the synagogue.

The apostle's opening words convey his respect for the Athenians' obvious religious devotion, noting that they even had an altar "to an unknown god." He continues with confidence, "What therefore you worship as unknown, this I proclaim to you" (17:23). Paul goes on to speak about God as creator of all, and of the irrelevance of temples that cannot contain the divine reality, an argument that he himself first heard from Stephen and one that resulted in Stephen's death by stoning. God is near every person, accessible to all, and Paul even quotes one of the Stoic poets in support of this truth. It was Aratus of Soli in Cilicia, near Tarsus, who said, "For we too are [God's] offspring" (17:28). Only at the end does Paul allude to Jesus, and then not by name, but speaking of the one God appointed and raised from the dead. Although the mention of resurrection is difficult for some of the Stoics and Epicureans to swallow, many appreciate Paul's erudition and obvious respect for the Greek philosophical ways. He moves on, but some join his number, including "Dionysius the Areopagite and a woman named Damaris, and others with them" (17:34). Here in the very heart of Gentile territory, new Christians without any background in Judaism were brought to the faith through the preaching of the onetime opponent of Gentile inclusion.

> It was Aratus of Soli in Cilicia, near Tarsus, who said, "For we too are [God's] offspring." (17:28)

This is a turning point in Acts, and a new model of evangelism for Paul and all who would follow in his footsteps. Until this point, there was always an assumption of a religious background, so it was possible to use scriptural quotations and draw on a shared tradition when introducing the good news about Jesus to people. Even Stephen's otherwise radical sermon about breaking through the tradition of the temple still assumed a Jewish religious background on his listeners' part. Now, in Athens, it becomes clear that all such assumptions must be discarded. Using Jesus' own words from the Gospels, new wine has to be delivered in new wineskins! Paul the Jewish scholar now taps into another side of himself to communicate the good news to those who would not have appreciated or perhaps even understood the old way of evangelism. Paul recognizes this different context for ministry and embraces it. He does not insist on a religious education program for his listeners before he tells them of God's great love for them; instead, he meets them right where they are in their journey. He does not belittle them or their efforts at spirituality; he honors them and, in doing so, brings them further along.

Don't Be Afraid

Corinth, located on the Peloponnesian peninsula and boasting three good harbors, was a busy commercial city in Paul's day. Because of the isthmus that separated the eastern and western seas, a ship tramway would convey ships from one side to the other, giving Corinth a monopoly on the shipping trade. Corinth was also a noted center of architecture and the arts, and from earlier Phoenician inhabitants the city inherited a robust and varied religious and mythological life, including the cult of Aphrodite that was so closely associated with Corinth. Though originally considered of lesser stature than cities like Athens and Sparta, Corinth grew to become the wealthiest and most influential city before it was destroyed in 146 BCE. Exactly one century later Julius Caesar restored the city, and by the time Paul visited it, Corinth had once again become a prominent and flourishing center, where people of many and varied backgrounds settled or simply passed through.

It was in Corinth that Paul encountered a married couple who would become two of his closest colleagues. Aquila was a Jew originally from Pontus in Asia Minor, but more recently a refugee from Rome after the Emperor Claudius expelled all Jews from the city. Luke refers to his wife Prisca in an affectionate manner by using the diminutive version of her name, Priscilla. In Corinth, Aquila plied his trade as a tentmaker, and it was in this capacity that Paul sought him out, for Paul too was a tentmaker—"because he was of the same trade, he stayed with them, and they worked together (18:3). This might be surprising to some readers, who think of Paul only in terms of his training as a rabbi and Pharisee, but the fact is that most Jewish children were trained in some kind of work with their hands, so that they could always have some measure of independence. Paul makes much of this in his later letters, reminding his fellow believers that he has never been a burden on them, but rather takes care of his own needs.

Aquila and Priscilla were obviously persuaded by Paul's arguments about Christ, for soon Luke shows them both working beside him and then in his place when he eventually leaves Corinth. Thus his leadership team is increasing in number even Paul faces increasingly vehement opposition from his opponents in the synagogues.

It is worth interrupting at this point to say something about this now-familiar pattern we find in Luke of hostility to Paul's message from many of the Jews and a corresponding openness on the part of many Gentiles. Like his gospel, Acts is not simply a random collection of unrelated tales but rather a strategic document that moves with purpose from start to finish, addressing issues and situations that Luke and his readers were facing in their own time. In 70 CE, the temple in Jerusalem—the Second Temple, or Herod's Temple—was destroyed by the Romans, never to be rebuilt to this day. The original temple was built during the reign of Solomon, David's son, and destroyed by the Babylonians in 586 BCE. The Second Temple was begun after the return from exile and then renovated by Herod the Great around 20 BCE. This crucial event in the history of Judaism meant that groups closely associated with temple worship, such as the Sadducees, simply ceased to exist. Others, like the Zealots, were beaten down by the Romans until they, too, died out. The two primary Jewish subgroups to survive the temple's destruction were those who learned to adapt without it. One group would evolve into rabbinic Judaism, bound together by study of the Torah and other sacred texts. The other group, of course, was the followers of Jesus. The first group emphasized separateness from Gentiles in order to preserve the community of faith. As we have seen, thanks to Paul and his colleagues, that other group embraced Gentiles and incorporated them together with Jewish Christians into something quite new. These two groups that survived the temple's destruction thus took different paths toward God. For the original readers of Acts, then, the primary rival for the local Christian church was often the synagogue down the street.

It is little wonder, then, that in his gospel Luke depicts Jesus experiencing constant antagonism from the Pharisees, the prototypes

> The original temple was built during the reign of Solomon, David's son, and destroyed by the Babylonians in 586 BCE. The Second Temple was begun after the return from exile and then renovated by Herod the Great around 20 BCE.

for the synagogue leaders and rabbinic teachers in Luke's own world. For Jewish Christians reading Luke's gospel and the book of Acts, the prophecies of Jesus about the eventual destruction of the temple must have been particularly poignant, since for them that destruction had already occurred. Likewise, the ongoing hostility Paul encountered would simply confirm for those same readers that the opposition they themselves faced was nothing new. In this sense, God's words to Paul in a vision are also directed to readers who experience similar hatred and hostility: "Do not be afraid; but speak and do not be silent; for I am with you, and no one will lay a hand on you to harm you, for there are many in this city who are my people" (18:9–10). As Paul found new converts in Corinth like Titius Justus and Crispus, so Luke's readers would make new friends and not just enemies.

A Need for Clarity—and Brevity

Following Paul's departure from Corinth, he moved fairly quickly through Ephesus, leaving behind Priscilla and Aquila, who encountered a charismatic preacher by the name of Apollos. This native of Alexandria is subsequently known for his (unwitting?) part in the partisanship that Paul combats in his first letter to the Corinthians. The description of Apollos in Acts as an "eloquent man, well-versed in the scriptures" who speaks with "burning enthusiasm" (18:24–25) gives credence to why a group of people later would claim, "I belong to Apollos" even as others said the same about Paul and Peter (1 Cor. 3:3). At the same time, we are told in Acts that Apollos is aware only of "the baptism of John." This is an interesting comment, and one not easily understood two thousand years later. Inasmuch as the apostles in Acts are described as those who proclaimed the resurrection of Christ, perhaps this is the deficiency to which Luke alludes about Apollos. In any case, it is significant that Paul's new colleagues, Priscilla and Aquila, have taken Apollos aside and "explained the Way of God to him more accurately," (18:26) thereby enhancing his ministry while also affirming it as he continues to reveal through the Hebrew Scriptures how Jesus was the prophesied Messiah.

Luke continues this train of thought as he describes Paul's encounter with believers in Ephesus who tell him they have been baptized "into

John's baptism" but who were completely unaware of the Holy Spirit. Paul explains to them, John baptized with the baptism of repentance, telling the people to believe in the one who was to come after him, that is, in Jesus" (19:4); he baptizes them in the name of Jesus and lays hands on them. At that point, Luke tells us, they began to speak in tongues and prophesy. This passage has been used in more recent centuries by those who emphasize the need for Christians to have a "second baptism" and glossolalia, the gift of speaking in ecstatic tongues. However, given Paul's assertion in 1 Corinthians that he "would rather speak five words with my mind . . . than ten thousand words in a tongue (1 Cor. 14:19), it is hard to imagine that here in Acts Paul would be depicted as advocating the very thing he argues against. More likely, Luke is making a connection between this passage and Acts 2, as this new set of potential leaders in Ephesus is filled with the Spirit for the purpose of gospel proclamation in tongues that others understand. It is probably not a coincidence that there were twelve of them (19:7).

Like Peter before him, during his two years in Ephesus Paul displays miraculous power, so much so that some "itinerant Jewish exorcists" begin casting out evil spirits by saying, "I adjure you by the Jesus whom Paul proclaims" (19:13). Seven sons of Sceva tried this, only to discover some very unhappy results. "Jesus I know, and Paul I know, but who are you?" the evil spirit asked the would-be exorcists before attacking them. Another riot that broke out during his time in Ephesus had to do with the worship of idols. Ephesus was the home of the great temple of Artemis, and the disturbance was initiated by an unhappy silversmith named Demetrius. He realizes that Paul's preaching is having a bad effect on his lucrative business of manufacturing idols for popular devotion. Artemis, Demetrius warns, will be "deprived of her majesty that brought all Asia and the world to worship her" (19:27), to say nothing of purchasing his wares. Interestingly, it was a town clerk who saved Paul from the mob this time(19:35—41), using the same calm reasoning that Gamaliel employed with the Jewish Council several years before.

More and more plots against Paul's life began to emerge, and his travel plans had to be adjusted accordingly. Through it all, his companions stayed with him and increased in number. At one point,

Luke lists a group that includes not only Timothy but also new and unfamiliar individuals who came from many of the places in which Paul had preached. There was Sopater from Boroea, Aristarchus and Secundus from Thessalonica, Gaius from Derbe, and Tychicus and Trophimus from Asia (20:4). It is not inconsequential that Gentile names now showed up more often than Jewish names.

Before beginning the long "passion narrative" of Paul that takes up the remainder of Acts, Luke offers one more view of Paul as one who encouraged and empowered others. The scene is a farewell to the Ephesian elders, presumably the twelve mentioned earlier. Here is the apostle's personal apologia, his testimony that he has done all that he could and is prepared for whatever will come next. Paul acknowledges to the elders his awareness that "imprisonments and persecutions are waiting for me" (20:23), but he remains resolute about moving forward and equally determined that these elders whom he has appointed will faithfully continue the work he began. Paul warns,

> I know that after I have gone, savage wolves will come in among you, not sparing the flock. Some even from your own group will come distorting the truth in order to entice the disciples to follow them. Therefore be alert, remembering that for three years I did not cease night or day to warn everyone with tears. (20:29–31)

His words about wolves stealing in echo the words of Jesus in Luke's gospel to the Twelve and to the Seventy who would carry on his own work. Like Jesus, Paul declares that he has worked tirelessly among them "for three years" and often with tears. The apostolic tentmaker asserts that he has earned his own living without being dependent on any of them, and offers a quotation of Jesus found only here and not in the gospels: "It is more blessed to give than to receive" (20:35).

As Paul took his leave of the elders in Ephesus, it is not difficult to see that these words were for Luke's own audience as well. It will be their job—and ours also—to continue the work that the apostle first began. Finishing his words, Paul knelt and prayed with them . . . and with Luke's readers and with us. The elders knew what Luke's readers already knew—and what we ourselves know—that Paul was preparing for his own passion and death, that they would never see him again. In a simple, powerful sentence, Luke notes that "they brought him to the ship" (20:38), and Paul began the final journey that would take him and the gospel of Jesus Christ to the ends of the earth.

CHAPTER 7

Apostolic Champion

*O God, by the preaching of your apostle
Paul you have caused the light of the
Gospel to shine throughout the world.*

COLLECT FOR THE CONVERSION OF SAINT PAUL,
THE BOOK OF COMMON PRAYER

It has often been said that the gospel accounts of Jesus
are really passion narratives with long introductions. Of
course this is not completely accurate, for where would the
Gospel according to Luke be without such jewels as the
parables of the Prodigal Son and the Good Samaritan, or
even the nativity story? These are hardly just filler material.
It is true, however, that everything in the gospel accounts
leads up to the climatic section surrounding the passion of
Jesus—his arrest, trial, crucifixion, death, and resurrection. In a similar way, Acts has been leading up to the final
lengthy section that is, in effect, Paul's "passion." It does
not end with his death, as will be discussed at the end of
this chapter, but there are otherwise some clear connections between Paul's journey to Rome and what awaits him
there, and the journey of Jesus towards his fate in
Jerusalem. There are other parallels to the heroic journey
and shipwreck that we find in this final section of Acts. We
have only to think of Homer's Odysseus, for example.
Finally, perhaps it goes without saying, but clearly the Acts
of the Apostles has evolved into the acts of the one apostle,
Paul. Luke's protagonist has not only taken center stage

above Peter, John, Stephen, Philip, and Barnabas, but his story now enters the realm of legend, a particularly impressive feat considering its unlikely beginnings.

To Jerusalem

For Luke, it always comes back to Jerusalem. Toward Jerusalem Jesus set his countenance and made his way. In Jerusalem the Holy Spirit descended and turned anxious followers into bold heralds. From Jerusalem the good news was carried forth throughout Judea and Samaria by a new set of witnesses. And now to Jerusalem comes Paul one last time. As in the case of Jesus, those who are close to Paul urge him not to go there, fearing his arrest or worse. In a fascinating verse, Luke even notes that the disciples in Tyre "through the Spirit" tell Paul not to go on. Yet he does, accompanied by his colleagues, including the author: "When our days there were ended, we left and proceeded on our journey" (21.4–5). They sail on from Tyre and along the way, old faces appear once again, such as Philip the evangelist, still living in Caesarea where we saw him last. Paul and company stay with him and his "four unmarried daughters who had the gift of prophecy" (21:9). Agabus also reappears. Though it is not explicitly stated, it is assumed that this Agabus is the same prophet who predicted the famine that resulted in Barnabas and Paul bringing financial assistance to the believers in Jerusalem. In any case, during their stay at Philip's home, a prophet named Agabus visits and offers a far more personal prophecy. Taking Paul's own belt, Agabus binds the apostle's hands and feet, saying, "This is the way the Jews in Jerusalem will bind the man who owns this belt and will hand him over to the Gentiles." Again Paul's traveling companions, including Luke, beg him not to go, and this time he clearly states his willingness to die for the name of Jesus. In Gethsemane, with the apostles dozing, it was Jesus alone who confessed, "Your will be done," but here Paul's friends, perhaps reluctantly, nevertheless agree: "The Lord's will be done" (21:11–14).

Once in Jerusalem Paul meets with James and the elders, with no more mention at all of Peter or the Twelve exercising any leadership

> Though it is not explicitly stated, it is assumed that this Agabus is the same prophet who predicted the famine that resulted in Barnabas and Paul bringing financial assistance to the believers in Jerusalem.

in the church there. Although he and his colleagues are welcomed warmly, it quickly becomes apparent that, to the elders there, Paul is still a dangerous person. After he relates his missionary success among the Gentiles, their anxiety reveals itself. Paul's opponents in Jerusalem have been saying that Paul teaches "all the Jews living among the Gentiles to forsake Moses and not to circumcise their children or observe the customs" (21:21). Rather than defend Paul to his adversaries, these nervous elders asked him to prove himself by sponsoring and visibly joining four Nazirites in a purification ritual. A Nazirite, or "consecrated one," took a vow of separation and self-imposed discipline as specified in Numbers 6:1–21. A Nazarite avoided wine and strong drink, had no contact with the dead, and did not cut his hair.

A Nazirite, or "consecrated one," took a vow of separation and self-imposed discipline as specified in Numbers 6:1–21. A Nazarite avoided wine and strong drink, had no contact with the dead, and did not cut his hair.

But the gambit does not work. Before the seven days of the ritual are even completed, while he is still in the temple, Paul is accosted by an angry crowd who accuse him of profaning the sacred site by bringing Gentiles onto the premises. Accusations soon turn into beatings, which cease only when soldiers come and take hold of him. Reminiscent of another crowd not many years before who repeatedly shouted out, "Crucify him!" this mob cried out against Paul over and over, "Away with him!" (v. 36). James and the elders have apparently underestimated the hostility of Paul's opponents. What is more amazing, however, is that there is no mention of the elders coming to Paul's defense. Instead, like the apostles at the time of Jesus' arrest, they all seem to have left him on his own.

Paul addresses the crowd directly, making his defense in Hebrew, offering his credentials as a pupil of Gamaliel's, admitting his previous hatred of the Way, and then recounting his own conversion. To that story Paul adds small but significant details not found originally in Luke's original; for example his description of his rescue by Ananias makes clear that this was not simply a disciple of Jesus, but also a devout follower of the Jewish law. Paul's report of a vision is new information, as well, showing how Jesus warned him in advance that those in Jerusalem would not listen to him, despite his credentials. "Go," Jesus told him, "for I will send you far away to the Gentiles"

(22:21). The crowd is inflamed; everything else Paul has said to that point becomes irrelevant as again they cry out for his death. To save him, the soldiers take Paul to the barracks.

At this point Luke gives us a fascinating interchange that will have significant ramifications for the apostle. As the soldiers are tying him up and preparing to flog him in order to get more information about the charges against them, Paul lets them know that they are about to flog a Roman citizen. Citizenship in the first century was a valuable, highly desired privilege. As the tribune's claim illustrates, citizenship could be purchased at a high price, but Paul the prisoner had actually been born a Roman citizen. This is, of course, the source of his Roman name, Paulus, alongside his Hebrew name of Saul. "Immediately those who were about to examine him drew back from him; and the tribune also was afraid" (22:29).

What follows is another echo of the passion of Jesus, specifically his trial before the Sanhedrin. Paul again has to defend himself, unwittingly insulting the High Priest in the process, and finally setting the council's members at odds with one another. Paul announces that he is on trial for his faith in the resurrection of the dead, a doctrine that is accepted by the Pharisees on the one hand but rejected by the Sadducees on the other. In the melee that follows, Paul once again has to be rescued by the Roman soldiers. When it becomes clear that an actual plot is underway to ambush and kill Paul, the tribune quietly makes provisions to get Paul out of the city once and for all, thanks in part to a word of warning from Paul's nephew. With this, Luke's account at long last leaves Jerusalem behind and moves us, his readers, one step closer to the ultimate destination of Rome.

Paul's Appeal

In the middle of the first century, the emperor Claudius appointed Felix Antonius as procurator, or governor, of Judea. It is to Felix that the soldiers bring Paul. Like Pontius Pilate before him, the governor has little desire to dirty his hands with an intra-religious controversy. For his part, Paul asserts that he has always done his best to have "a clear conscience toward God and all people" (24:16). So if he truly has committed a crime worthy of imprisonment or death, let his accusers come forward with evidence. They cannnot, of course, but instead simply let their accusing cries to the governor grow louder. Paul makes the most of every interview with Felix, "and as he discussed justice, self-control, and the coming judgment," Luke reports, "Felix became frightened and said, 'Go away for the present; when I have an opportunity, I will send for you'" (24:25). The governor was unnerved by Paul's words, and tries his best to bribe the apostle in order make a deal with him. Unsurprisingly, for Paul, bribes were out of the question. The prisoner outlasted the career bureaucrat, and soon it is to the next governor, Porcius Festus, that the apostle's enemies come with their charges. As with Felix, again Paul asserts his innocence, only to be faced with the possibility of returning to Jerusalem for trial, hardly an attractive option, as it would almost certainly end with Paul's death. There is only one thing to do, and Paul appeals to the emperor himself.

Even as the tragic event of Stephen's death had the unexpected benefit of the spread of the gospel through the dispersion of believers, so Paul's enemies unwittingly allowed him to realize his greatest dream. The gospel will now go to Rome itself as a result of his appeal to the emperor. This could not have happened with Peter or John, for they were simply Galilean fishermen-turned-preachers. Paul of Tarsus, however, is a Roman citizen, born with the rights of citizenship, including the right to appeal for justice to a higher court, even to Caesar himself. For a long time "Rabbi Saul" has distanced himself from his own Roman heritage, but now the former pupil of Gamaliel's will embrace this other side of himself. He truly has become the "Apostle to the Gentiles."

Of course, it will take time to prepare for the journey to Rome. Before their departure, Festus allows Herod Agrippa to interview Paul; once again Paul relates the story of his former life and his conversion. In each new telling of the story of Paul's metamorphosis from persecutor to promulgator of the faith, new details emerge. It is interesting to view Luke's three accounts of what Saul actually hears at the moment of his encounter with Christ:

"Saul, Saul, why do you persecute me?" He asked, "Who are you, Lord?" The reply came, "I am Jesus, whom you are persecuting. But get up and enter the city, and you will be told what you are to do." (Acts 9:4–6)

"Saul, Saul, why are you persecuting me?" I answered, "Who are you, Lord?" Then he said to me, "I am Jesus of Nazareth* whom you are persecuting." Now those who were with me saw the light but did not hear the voice of the one who was speaking to me. I asked, "What am I to do, Lord?" The Lord said to me, "Get up and go to Damascus; there you will be told everything that has been assigned to you to do." (Acts 22:7–10)

I heard a voice saying to me in the Hebrew* language, "Saul, Saul, why are you persecuting me? It hurts you to kick against the goads." I asked, "Who are you, Lord?" The Lord answered, "I am Jesus whom you are persecuting. But get up and stand on your feet; for I have appeared to you for this purpose, to appoint you to serve and testify to the things in which you have seen me* and to those in which I will appear to you. I will rescue you from your people and from the Gentiles—to whom I am sending you to open their eyes so that they may turn from darkness to light and from the power of Satan to God, so that they may receive forgiveness of sins and a place among those who are sanctified by faith in me." (Acts 26:14–18)

In this latest retelling of his conversion, Paul actually goes on for some time with the quotation from Jesus, explaining the purpose for God's call: "So that they may turn from darkness to light and from the power of Satan to God, so that they may receive forgiveness of sins and a place among those who are sanctified by faith in me." This version of the conversion story, told to King Agrippa, is explicit in the commission to do apostolic work among the Gentiles, but it is also balanced by Paul's own assertion that he is "saying nothing but what the prophets and Moses said would take place." Thus Paul is quick to base the Gentile mission in the sacred tradition of Judaism. Then Paul turns the full force of his oratory directly on King Agrippa: "Do you believe the prophets? I know that you believe." The king's response shows just how much he did understand Paul: "Are you so quickly persuading me to become a Christian" (v. 28)? The apostle's retort, echoing sentiments found in his own letters written during his final years of imprisonment, has a poignancy that carries through the years and reveals why he remains the hero of Luke's narrative: "Whether quickly or not, I pray to God that not only you but also all who are listening to me today might become such as I am—except for these chains" (6:22–29).

The invitation to faith in Christ despite the visible hardships it brings is also Luke's invitation to his readers. Indeed, Luke's original audience would have heard these words spoken in the context of a worship service and thus could be included among "all who are listening to me today." This invitation still rings forth, for it reminds all today who would have ears to hear that Christianity has never been a "pie in the sky" religion. From the start Christians have acknowledged that the road of faith would not be an easy one, but will involve heartache and even bloodshed. Leaving the scene, both Gentile governor and Jewish ruler agree that Paul has done nothing to deserve death or imprisonment, and in this observation subsequent Christian readers are reminded that the same is true for them. And the God who gave Paul the strength to endure would be there for them—for us—as well.

Paul's Odyssey

If the previous story on Paul's arrest and the various venues of his defense recall the passion narrative of Luke's gospel, here the tales diverge and the apostle's adventures parallel the travels of Homer's Odysseus rather than Jesus' journey to the cross. It begins with a sea voyage to Rome, the imperial capital, center of the universe for many and the ends of the earth for others. The author explicitly enters the scene again, recounting that "we" set sail for Italy, on a ship of Adramyttium, a seaport of Mysia in Asia Minor. Paul the prisoner and his team are joined by Aristarchus, a Macedonian from Thessalonica. Aristarchus appears earlier in Acts and, along with Gaius, was manhandled by an angry crowd during the riot in Ephesus (19:29). He was not dissuaded from sharing with Paul in the apostolic mission.

As we the readers sail with Paul and his colleagues, we speed past many places. Some are familiar—like Sidon, from where a delegation once came to make an appeal to Herod Agrippa I (12:20) and where now the supervising centurion allows Paul to see his friends (27:3)—and others are unfamiliar, like Myra (27:5), mentioned only here in the New Testament, but later linked forever with the patron saint of children, Saint Nicholas. With the winds against them, sailing becomes difficult and time is lost. Paul warns his captors that if they continue their journey, there will be much loss of life and property. Perhaps predictably, the centurion does not listen to Paul but at the advice of the ship's captain and crew pressed on, setting the stage for disaster.

Disaster arrives in the form of "a violent wind called the northeaster" from Crete, which seizes control of the ship and drives it on towards certain doom. Amidst the storm's battering, even the ship's tackle is thrown overboard as the passengers despair: "When neither sun nor stars appeared for many days, and no small tempest raged, all hope of our being saved was at last abandoned" (27:20). Only Paul remains calm. After a wonderful moment in which he reminds everyone that they should have taken his advice, the apostle urges all aboard to eat and take comfort, for an angel of God has revealed to him in a vision that he will indeed stand before the emperor in Rome, and all who sail with him have been granted safety.

Luke's detailed and dramatic description of the sailors' work, not to mention enticing nuggets such as the attempt by some cowardly crew members to take a few lifeboats and leave the ship, allows readers to experience the wind and the waves alongside Paul. Luke's use of "we" not only signals his own participation in events, but in a real way includes us, the readers. We, too, are there amidst the chaos and danger and terror of the moment. We can almost hear the sickening sound of wood being torn apart as, running aground on a reef, the bow became stuck and the stern continued to be pummeled and ultimately broken apart. Despite the guards' desire to kill the prisoners in order to prevent their escape in the melee, the centurion orders that all who can swim to land should do so, followed by others hanging onto planks or other debris. "And so it was that all were brought safely to land" (v. 44). The island on which they found themselves was called Malta.

Luke notes the kindness and gentle welcome granted to the shipwrecked party by the natives of the island. Not unlike the crowds in

Lystra who, witnessing the healing of a crippled man, declared Paul and Barnabas to be gods come down in human form, so now the islanders believe Paul to be divine after he was bitten by a viper: They were expecting him to swell up or drop dead, but after they had waited a long time and saw that nothing unusual had happened to him, they changed their minds and began to say that he was a god (28:6). Other healings follow, and the inhabitants show their appreciation, eventually giving Paul and the rest of the ship's company a munificent send-off. (It is ironic that Paul found greater hospitality and welcome from these islanders than he did from his own kin.) Paul and the rest set sail on another Alexandrian ship that had wintered at Malta, this one having as its figurehead the Dioskoúrois, the "Twin Brothers" or "Sons of Zeus" (28:11). Born of Zeus and Leda, the mythological brothers Castor and Pollux were together the patron deities of sailors. Resuming their journey, they came to Syracuse in Sicily, where they stayed briefly, before crossing over into Italy itself.

> Born of Zeus and Leda, the mythological brothers Castor and Pollux were together the patron deities of sailors.

The ship landed at Puteoli, literally meaning "little wells," referring to the many sulfur springs in the area on account of the volcanic formation that marked the region. With roots going back to Hannibal two centuries before the coming of Christ, the town became the first Roman port on the Gulf of Naples and indeed the chief port of the capital for many years. Cicero had a villa in the surrounding region, which was later used as Hadrian's burial site. There is no mention of how the Christian faith first came to that place, only that Paul found a group of believers already there when he arrived. Now only 140 miles separate the apostle from his ultimate destination. After staying a week in Puteoli and then making their way north along the famous Appian Way, Luke finally reports, with familiar understatement, "And so we came to Rome" (28:14).

Once in Rome Paul was granted very generous privileges, living under house arrest and able to host others in his home. Not surprisingly, the first group he calls together are the local Jewish leaders as part of his attempt to make one more defense before them. Paul assures them that he means no harm to his fellow Jews, even claiming that it was "for the sake of the hope of Israel" that he was bound and imprisoned. Many come to his lodgings and Paul spends the day arguing from the law of Moses and the prophets that Jesus is the promised Messiah. In the end, "some were convinced by what he had said, while others refused to believe" (28:24). As the religious leaders leave the house debating with one another, Paul—and ultimately, the author of Acts—lets loose one more reminder that, even if they will not believe, there are Gentiles who will: "Let it be known to you then that this salvation of God has been sent to the Gentiles; they will listen." It is Paul's last word in Acts. But Luke has an important epilogue to share.

The Final Act

The two final verses of the book of Acts summarize the remainder of Paul's life in Rome: "He lived there two whole years at his own expense and welcomed all who came to him, proclaiming the kingdom of God and teaching about the Lord Jesus Christ with all boldness and without hindrance" (28:30—31). Many readers through the centuries have struggled with the open-endedness of this finale. For those who want to learn about the end of Paul's life on earth, they have to go outside of Acts and even beyond the New Testament to late first-century Christian tradition about the deaths of Peter and Paul. It is said that Paul, as well as Simon Peter, was martyred in the time of the Emperor Nero. While Peter was crucified, Paul, being a Roman citizen, was beheaded on the Ostian Road outside Rome, which was considered a more merciful death.

In the New Testament itself, Paul's letter to the Philippians is one of his last epistles, written while he was in prison and believing himself soon to face execution. There he speaks of his willingness to leave this world and be with Christ (Phil. 1:23), though he also acknowledges that there is still work for him to do here. 2 Timothy, an epistle attributed to Paul but more likely written later, has a nice touch of placing Luke still with Paul in his final imprisonment, as well as the apostle's desire to be reunited with John Mark, whose departure had been the source of the division between Paul and Barnabas (2 Tim. 4:11). That same epistle contains final words that might well go back to Paul himself, and certainly reflect the spirit of his life and ministry: "As for me, I am already being poured out as a libation, and the time of my departure has come. I have fought the good fight, I have finished the course, I have kept the faith" (4:6). Although there is no one passage in or after the New Testament that describes the actual martyrdom of Paul of Tarsus, there is little doubt that the apostle did indeed meet his end with courage, faith, and conviction.

But it is not Paul's death, but rather his apostolic witness to Christ, that is the last word in Acts. Instead, what some see as an open-ended finale is actually an invitation to all who have followed the apostle's story from Jerusalem to Rome, to claim their apostolic heritage and continue the work that they began. It is an invitation to proclaim the reign of God, to teach all who will listen about Jesus Christ, and to do so boldly. It is an invitation to take Luke's account and add our own new chapters, not with ink on papyrus or paper but with our lives. The players in Acts may have left the stage, but two thousand years later we who follow Christ still have our part to play onstage. The final curtain has not yet closed, and the final chapter of Acts is still being written.

ACKNOWLEDGMENTS

It is a pleasure to work again with Church Publishing, this time in the thought-provoking "Conversations with Scripture" series in its Morehouse imprint. Once more, I give thanks for the wise and very helpful input of my editor, Cynthia Shattuck.

In many ways, this book is the outgrowth of my years of doctoral study at Durham University in England. To Professor James D. G. Dunn and all my colleagues there, especially Doug Mohrmann, B.J. Oropeza, and James McGrath, I offer my appreciation.

During the time of this writing and editing, I had the pleasure of teaching a course on Acts at the General Theological Seminary. I deeply appreciate the many ways in which my students took seriously their own part in the "conversation" with Acts, and was challenged and encouraged by what I heard from them.

I remain so grateful for the support of the Most Rev. Katharine Jefferts Schori, as well as my colleagues in the Office of the Presiding Bishop: Ednice Baerga, Miguel Escobar, Yvonne O'Neal, Sharon Jones, Su Hadden, the Hon. Linda Watt and the Rt. Rev. Herbert Donovan.

I also am awed by the care and encouragement I continue to experience from my family: Teri and Rich Ridler, Pam and Frank Valant, Fred, Lou and Deirdre Robertson, Robin and Katherine Robertson, and Bill and Pat Vinson. I also give thanks for my dear friends who know me so well and yet continue to stand with me, especially Gary and Laurie Reichard, Kevin and Helen Jamison, Mike Maichak, and Kirk and Laura Smith, Michael and Gill Rusk, Jack and Marianne Joris, and Mike and Diane Rhodes.

And, of course, I give such deep and abiding thanks for the continued support of Debbie, David, Jonathan, and Abigail.

STUDY QUESTIONS

by Sharon Ely Pearson

The Acts of the Apostles is one of the most exciting and action-packed books in the Christian Testament. Here we hear the evocative story of the Church's roots that traces its beginnings in the final days of the risen Jesus and the Pentecostal arrival of the Holy Spirit, to Paul's final missionary trip to Rome. Chuck Robertson takes us on a journey of how the good news of Jesus Christ spread from Jerusalem to the "ends of the earth" from the viewpoint that we too are called to be apostles. Meeting these first Christians and experiencing their passion and struggles among Jews and Gentiles gives us a glimpse of what it means to be a follower of Christ. As Robertson states, "Acts is an utterly incarnational book" that focuses on "flesh and blood heralds and heroes, the fragile, fallible, altogether human people." He explores this apostolic period descriptively and alliteratively: call, concord, challenge, change, compromise, colleagues, and champion. While this story ends in Rome, we are encouraged to continue to be witnesses in our own time. We may choose to see how these words with a "c" apply to our own lives and ministry.

Introduction

This study guide is meant to accompany each chapter as a means to go deeper and reflect upon the events, personalities, and ideas that the author unpacks through the chapters of Acts. The questions and reflections will invite you into a conversation about the role of an apostle—in the first century and in today's world. How we connect with Peter and Paul as well as all their compatriots can help us discern how we might be followers of "the Way" in the twenty-first century.

The Acts of the Apostles describes the deeds of the first Christians with a focus on two major figures: Peter (who is one of the twelve apostles, and appears at first with John) is prominent in ten chapters, while Paul (who is only twice called an apostle, and appears at first with Barnabas) is prominent in seventeen chapters. Written in approximately 85 CE to churches affected directly or indirectly (through others) by Paul's missionary journeys, Luke (through Robertson's understanding) takes us through a cast of characters, and their interactions with one another, as we are witnesses to a plot that any movie director would seize to re-enact. You are invited not only to become the audience, but also be co-participants in the mission.

As you begin this study of Acts, consider the following:
- Why are you engaging in this study of Acts of the Apostles?
- What have your previous understandings and opinions of Peter, Paul, and the other apostles been? Do you go into this study with any preconceived notions? If so, jot them down before reading.
- What do you hope to learn and discern for yourself in this study?
- What is the Greco-Roman world like at this period of our world's history? How is it different to today's world? Similar?

Before each chapter of this book, portions of Scripture will be suggested to read ahead of time. You may also wish to have at hand a map of the Roman world as well as one depicting Paul's journeys. These can be found in the appendix of most study bibles.

Chapter One: Apostolic Call

This first chapter sets the scene for our storyteller, Luke, and his probable patron, Theophilus. Robertson suggests that Theophilus may also have been a pupil of Luke's, a catechist who needed to "know the truth concerning the things about which you have been instructed" (Luke 1:14). So it is also with us, recipients of God's good news, beloved of God . . . only many generations removed. Is this a catechism by which new converts (then and now) might learn of God while participating in a religious movement following the risen Jesus?

Read Luke 24:1–53 and Acts 1:1–26

While we have four canonized versions of Jesus' life, death, and resurrection, we only have one account of what happened next. We don't know what was left out but we do get a sense of different viewpoints and opinions in the relationships we see between all the individuals involved in the early church. In Acts we have Luke's views, while later in Paul's letters, we can understand what these individuals faced in their perspective communities from his standpoint. Robertson suggests that Luke's story is for future generations, not just for the first century.

Some interpretive questions to ask while reading:
- How does Acts serve as a bridge between the four gospels and various epistles (letters by Paul and others) to tell the Christian story?
- What circumstances occasioned the writing of Acts?
- How did Luke compose the story of Acts? How is it different than the gospels?
- What does Acts teach us about God?
- What role does Acts continue to perform within the New Testament?
- What theological arguments are being raised?
- What are the essential points of faith for the earliest Christians? For us today?

Each chapter of this book focuses on an aspect of apostleship. Luke uses *apostolos* more than any other New Testament writer. Meaning "one who is sent (forth)" from the Greek verb "to send," Luke uses the term for those who are chosen by God to carry God's word to others (Luke 6:12–16).
- What are the attributes of an apostle?
- Who are these particular apostles sent forth to?
- How is an apostle trained for his (or her) mission?
- What would have been the main message of an apostle of Jesus Christ in the first century? Today?
- How were apostles chosen in the early church? Are any of these methods used today for the calling of leaders (lay or ordained)? What is your understanding of apostolic succession? Do you believe this has been a help or a hindrance for the Church?

Throughout the early chapters of Acts, Luke emphasizes that the new faith is grounded in Judaism . . . grounded in a call from God . . . and brought to life by the Holy Spirit.

- How do these first apostles live this out?
- Where is your faith grounded? In past traditions, persons, or places? In the present? Future?
- What would it mean for you to be an apostle of Jesus Christ?
- How do you recognize the call of God? The power of the Spirit? The model of Jesus?
- What do you believe about the Holy Spirit? How have you experienced the presence and work of the Holy Spirit in your life?

Chapter Two: Apostolic Concord

Robertson prefaces the story of Pentecost with recollections of "idyllic" times in the Hebrew Scriptures: the Garden of Eden, laying claim to the Promised Land, the golden age of David, and reign of Solomon. While we claim the Day of Pentecost as a Christian celebration, we must remember its roots—the Jewish feast of offering the first fruits of the harvest as well as a commemoration of receiving the Mosaic Law (Ten Commandments) at Mount Sinai. With these insights, he places our Feast of Pentecost in an interesting light:

- What are your first fruits?
- What harvest could they lead to?
- What do we glean and what do we leave behind (give) for others?
- By offering ourselves to God, how are we present (or not) for the coming of the Spirit?

Read Acts 2:1–13, Genesis 1:2; 2:7, I Kings 19:9–12, and Psalm 135:7

- What connections does Luke (and Robertson) make with these passages?
- What images do you associate with the Holy Spirit?
- What other instances in Scripture do you find the Spirit at work? How are these similar to Pentecost? Different?

Read Acts 2:14–47

The Spirit's dramatic arrival fulfills Jesus' prophecy (1:4–5), enabling the entire community to communicate God's word to the household of Israel. Suddenly Peter and the other apostles become "preaching dynamos." Where days and hours before the apostles were sequestered and fearful, they now are ready for action. The Christian community forms with purpose and power.

- What is needed when a new community is formed?
- What helps it to survive?
- What can threaten its survival?

The Episcopal Church's baptismal covenant (BCP, 304–5) continues this practice (2:43–47) today. Journal or discuss what these questions mean to you and how you live them out in your daily life (with God's help).

- Will you continue in the apostles' teaching and fellowship, in the breaking of bread, and in the prayers?
- Will you persevere in resisting evil, and, whenever you fall into sin, repent and return to the Lord?
- Will you proclaim by word and example the Good News of God in Christ?
- Will you seek and serve Christ in all persons, loving your neighbor as yourself?
- Will you strive for justice and peace among all people, and respect the dignity of every human being?

Read Acts 3:1—6:7

With the growth of any community, there come celebrations and challenges. This was no different in the early church. Robertson discusses several issues that served as essential—and unexpected—parts of their life together. Reflect on how these built up the community or caused anxiety in Luke's time. How do others view these values outside their community? Thinking of today, how is life in your church community (or any other community) addressing these same issues now? Give examples.

- Being of one heart and soul
- No private ownership of any possessions
- Interdependence among its members
- Generosity
- Fear
- Showing signs and wonders
- Offering the ministry of proclamation
- Failing to perform a commission
- Empowerment
- Increase in members
- Devotion to teaching and fellowship

The rapid growth in church membership also strained the administration in serving those most vulnerable to which they felt called. This goes to the heart of the community's public identity and occasioned the twelve apostles to reconsider their prophetic vocation— not to wait on tables but to boldly proclaim the word of God. By selecting "seven men of good standing," the community followed Jesus' pattern of sending out others. Robertson acknowledges the all-too-familiar limits of success. While the twelve remained in Jerusalem, Jesus' message is spreading . . .

- Was there a need for the Temple as the church grew? How tied are we to our institutional buildings in spreading the good news?
- What if the leaders had followed Gamaliel's principle of judging new developments instead of reacting in a hostile manner so quickly?
- What would have happened to the Jesus movement if it had remained a Jewish sectarian association?

Robertson tells a story of stewardship in discussing the role that money and possessions play in our life and church community. He says, "For Luke, the converted life is visibly represented by a radical new approach to one's treasures."

- How do you determine who is trustworthy for the keeping of treasures?
- How does the sharing of possessions exercise both spiritual and social leadership in a communal system?
- How are you (and your church community) stewards of your finances as well as one another?
- How does your community take care of its own members in need?
- How does one's possessions (or lack thereof) reveal a true and deep response to the gospel of Jesus?

Chapter Three: Apostolic Challenge

By the end of the previous chapter, Robertson laid the groundwork for the challenges facing this new apostolic community. No longer a homogenous group, there is tension between the Hellenists and the Hebrews who each consider themselves Jewish Christians. He believes the introduction of newcomers who are perceived as "different" to the community presents a problematic situation to the loving and sharing community of faith.

Read Acts 6:8—7:60

More questions of authority and the age-old problem of "those new-comers" continue to arise. Toleration dissolves, leading to persecution and then martyrdom. New leaders emerge from the original twelve—Stephen and Barnabas, in particular.

- Make a list of the difference between the Hellenists (Jews from the Diaspora who spoke Greek) and the Hebrews (Jews in and around Jerusalem who spoke Aramaic). What did they have in common? Why would one feel threatened by the other?
- How do you welcome the stranger?
- How do you view others "like" yourself? "Unlike" yourself?
- How can one preserve their heritage while also being inclusive of new ideas and influences?
- How is this seen in your own life or the church community today?
- What does this tell us of the possibility that the newcomer in our midst might have something to offer us?
- What happens when we open our doors to all?

With a growing community also comes the delegation of roles and tasks. Today we would call this one's call to ministry.

- When is it necessary to delegate responsibility?
- What are the characteristics of being a leader? Any requirements?
- What is your understanding of the *diakonia*?
- Does your church have a deacon? Why or why not? What is their role in the life of the worshipping community? Of the greater community?
- What is the role of a deacon in your church?
- What is the difference between "serving tables" and "serving the word"? Is one more important than the other? Why or why not?
- Are you called to either of these roles?

Read Acts 8:1–40

Stephen, Deacon and Martyr is commemorated on December 26, and Philip, Deacon and Evangelist on October 11. *Holy Women, Holy*

Men (Church Publishing, 2010) offers brief bibliographies of them as well as the appointed lessons for their day. As one of the "Seven," Stephen was assigned to table service as a deacon, but immediately began apostolic work by preaching to the Sanhedrin, which led to his stoning and ultimately to the spread of the *kerygma* beyond Jerusalem. Philip took on the mantle of Stephen as we see the expansion of the Christian mission take hold.

- Review the various types of leadership, parties, and their roles in the worshipping Jewish community: Sadducees, Sanhedrin, Priests, Pharisees, and Scribes. What could their role be in this new movement of Christians?
- Who were the Freedmen? Do we have any parallels to this class of people in our country or churches today?
- Stephen considered Moses God's prototypical prophet, who establishes the pattern of bringing God's word to Israel. What elements in his sermon upset each of the above parties? How would you have responded to his blasphemy?
- Robertson notes a sense of déjà vu with Stephen's sermon, accusations and stoning with the passion and death of Jesus. Make a list all of the similarities and differences. Why would Luke draw such parallels?
- Are there people in our recent history who have exemplified being a true witness of Christ? Do they share similar parallels?
- Have you ever been persecuted for your faith? What brought it on? How did you react? What does the absence of persecution indicate?

Robertson discusses the world *homothudón*, meaning "with one accord" and its frequent occurrence in Acts. This also appears in *A Prayer of St. Chrysostom* from Morning Prayer and Evening Prayer in the 1979 Book of Common Prayer:

> Almighty God, you have given us grace at this time with one accord to make our common supplication to you; and you have promised through your well-beloved Son that when two or three are gathered together in his Name you will be in the midst of them: Fulfill now, O Lord, our desires and petitions as may be best for us; granting us in this world knowledge of your truth, and in the age to come life everlasting. *Amen.*

- How does this prayer carry on a sense of the mission of Philip?
- How was the community "with one voice" detrimental to the apostolic mission? Does this ever happen today?

This chapter concludes with an examination of the commissioning and sending out of apostles. Robertson makes many comparisons from the occurrences in Acts with incidents in Jesus' ministry as well as parallels with Moses' prophetic ministry. Do you agree with him? What themes and connections to you find familiar in Acts that you have read in previous stories in the Bible?

Chapter Four: Apostolic Change

God's Spirit making bold witnesses out of ordinary people becomes the reason behind the phenomenal success of the first-generation church. Paul emerges as Acts' main character and leader in the ministry among the fastest growing segment of the church: non-Jews.

Read Acts 9:1—12:25

Peter now begins to fade in importance as Saul has a conversion on the road to Damascus. Robertson reviews a variety of stories that are familiar to many about Saul/Paul and Peter, exploring themes of change, call, inclusion, divine intervention, and prayer.

Learn more about the various characters in these chapters of Acts and how they understand their call to proclaim God's message. Visualize their remarkable experiences and the impact it has on their lives. In a small group, each take on one of the roles; how might these individuals converse with one another over an evening meal? What personalities do they bring to the table? What are their passions? What are their gifts for ministry? Which person do you relate to the most?

- Saul of Tarsus
- Gamaliel
- Ananias
- Peter
- Dorcas
- Cornelius
- Barnabas
- James, the brother of John
- James, the brother of Jesus

The call of Samuel (1 Samuel 3) comes to Robertson's mind when discussing Saul's conversion. He also states it is "as much about the conversions of other believers as it is about his." Both boy and man receive divine imperatives. How are their calls similar? Different? Blindness is also a theme in Scripture—in healings and conversions.

- Allegorically, do these stories have relevance to recognizing our call to follow God today?
- How would you answer a call in the night or along the road?
- Have you ever been blinded or seen things anew after an experience?
- How has Jesus changed your life?
- What special assignment might he be calling you to now?

The term "Christian" didn't surface until about a decade after Christ, perhaps as a demeaning term. The earliest Christians called themselves followers of "the Way," short for "the way of God." However, Peter and Paul had different views for who this new "way" was really for.

- How are we protective of our tradition and faith as Saul was? As Peter?
- Full inclusion meant breaking down barriers. What barriers need to be broken down today?
- Saul was considered a "dangerous one." Who do we consider our "dangerous ones"?
- Are there people in your world who seem outside the reach of the gospel?
- What could you do to build a bridge between them and the Good News?
- How do you feel about sharing your faith with others?
- How might God be at work in the lives of your unbelieving friends?
- How could you have a part in what God is doing?

The theme of this chapter is change. Robertson shares that "change does not come easily" and the world of the first believers was "turned upside down in ways they could not have imagined." How do you deal with change? Has change ever affected your faith?

Chapter Five: Apostolic Compromise

Saul begins traveling to new, growing congregations in Antioch (present-day Syria). With Barnabas, he begins a new phase of this missionary movement. Most of the new believers are non-Jews, bringing the first big controversy to the church. Observing the laws of Moses, especially those about circumcision and diet, were requirements in the "mother church" located in Jerusalem. Does one need to become a Jew to be a Christian?

Read Acts 13:1—15:41

Robertson recalls the opening chapter of Acts and how the apostles were commissioned. As Peter and the Twelve were apostles of Jerusalem, Barnabas and Saul are now apostles of Antioch and beyond. With the power of the Holy Spirit, following a time of prayer and fasting there was a laying-on of hands and a sending off. This pattern of commissioning continues in the church today. Review the following liturgies—what portions of these services are reminiscent of Acts? How are they similar to one another? Different? What parts have meaning to you?

- The Ordination of a Bishop (BCP pp. 512–23)
- The Ordination of a Priest (BCP pp. 525–35)
- The Ordination of a Deacon (BCP pp. 537–47)
- Confirmation (BCP pp. 413–19)
- Celebration of a New Ministry (BCP pp. 559–65)
- The Reconciliation of a Penitent (BCP pp. 447–52)

Saul comes to be known by his Roman name, Paul, marking this new change in his life. Throughout Scripture the naming of a person or object is an important symbol of ownership and acceptance. Names often also describe a characteristic of a person or place. As Paul, he begins to take the good news of Jesus Christ to "the ends of the earth."

- Why did Paul change his name?
- Have you ever changed your name or took on a new name? What did this mean to you?
- Have you ever named someone? How did you choose the name?
- What characteristics does Paul have for the work that lay ahead of him?
- What characteristics does Barnabas have for mission?
- What made people believe Paul?
- Why does Paul have to defend his apostleship in some places and not in others? Have you ever found yourself in a similar situation?
- How are Peter's and Paul's experiences of healing and preaching similar, despite the difference of their audiences?

The further Paul traveled from Jerusalem, the less his audience understood the Scriptures as a Jewish audience naturally would. Reaching a different kind of people who had not been brought up in the faith of Israel was a new challenge for Paul, as the concept of worshipping one God was foreign to them.

- As more and more people are not "churched" today, how might we model ourselves on Paul's style?
- How do you speak of God and Jesus to those who do not believe or who have never heard of them?
- How do we share the gospel to people who have no religious training?
- How do we train others to share the gospel?

Examine the orders of ministry that begin to occur in the new churches. How are they forerunners of ordained ministry today?

- Presbyters / Elders
- Apostles
- Deacons
- Evangelists / Church Planters

When a disagreement became public within the new communities, the opponents didn't revert to gossip or infighting. At the First Jerusalem Council, they came together, listened to all sides, remained sensitive to the Holy Spirit, and compromised. Robertson says, "There have always been some who have argued that something more is needed beyond God's grace and our response of faith."

- What were the issues faced by these communities?
- What were the roots of the importance of dietary laws and circumcision in Jewish communities?
- Why did Paul (and others) feel they were unnecessary to new converts?
- What issues has the church faced throughout history? How were they resolved (or not)?
- What arguments do we face in our communities today? How would Paul respond? Peter? (Think about their characteristics and passion as described by Robertson, not particular passages of Scripture that may be taken out of context.)

Barnabas and Paul depart company. According to Robertson it is because Barnabas became a liability.

- In what ways? Do you agree, or not?
- How does Paul's mission change (or not) without Barnabas?
- Have you ever parted from a colleague or vocation due to a disagreement?

- What are the roles of companions on a journey or mission?

Chapter Six: Apostolic Colleagues

Paul continues his missionary efforts, partnering with new companions after his separation with Barnabas. He travels beyond Roman Asia to the Diaspora Jews and the Gentiles. For Paul, apostolic ministry is not a solo effort. To further your study, you may wish to read any of the epistles (letters) that Paul (or his fellow travelers) wrote to the churches they visited or established along the way.

Read Acts 16:1—18:21

Paul continues to find new apprentices along his second journey. Use a map from a study bible to locate all these new church plants. Robertson states that they often "hit a wall" as they attempt to move further east into Asia.

- Why does Paul wish to go into Asia?
- How did Paul determine which cities to go to? Do they have anything in common?
- What obstacles or "walls" do you think they encountered?
- What helps them proceed and not give up in their mission?
- How does the existence of the Roman Empire assist Paul in his journeys?
- Paul seems to be the right man, at the right time in world history. But how is his personality suited to the task? Do you agree with Robertson's translation?
- How does God use our detours to get us where we need to be?

Learn more about each of these individuals who become his colleagues: What are the characteristics that Paul discovers in each of them? How are they included into the faith? Are there any obstacles that must be overcome? How do they add to building up the Body of Christ?

- Silas
- Timothy
- Lydia (Is she the female equivalent of Cornelius that we learned of in Chapter 10?)
- The Jailer at Philippi
- Aquila
- Priscilla

- Jason
- Titius Justus
- Crispus
- Apollos

Paul and Silas are often confronted and jailed. Robertson names several of the charges brought against them.

- What would you name as the charges?
- Would Paul and his colleagues be considered dangerous in today's world? If so, how? If not, what is different today?
- What role does the synagogue play in Paul's various stops along the way?
- When riots occur in our time, what are some of the causes? Are there any parallels to the first-century issues?
- As a Christian, how would you respond? How do you decide which "side" to take?

Athens was a major hub of civilization in the world. It was a pagan city where Paul faced those who followed Epicurean and Stoic philosophy. Research these philosophies to see how they differed from Christianity as well as what they had in common. According to Robertson, these were considered very practical and life-affirming belief systems.

- What similar belief systems do we find in our world today?
- What are the gods of our world in the twenty-first century that Paul would have addressed?
- How is Paul able to key his message to the audience at hand? What can we learn from him?
- What is the new model of evangelism for Paul?
- What can we learn about developing religious education programs for today's church from his experience in Athens?

Robertson states that "Acts is not simply a random collection of unrelated tales but rather a strategic document that moves with purpose from start to finish addressing issues and situations that Luke and his readers were facing in their own time."

- Develop a strategic plan that Paul might have conceived before each of his missionary journeys.
- Develop a strategic plan for your church to proclaim the good news of Jesus. What contingency plans do you have for when you need to follow another path?

■ How do you react when faced with hatred and hostility about something you believe in? Can you learn anything from Paul's example?

This chapter concludes with Paul leaving Ephesus to prepare for his last journey. Robertson reminds us that the job of the apostles is left to the Ephesians—and us. What would Paul say to you as he left your home or community after a visit?

Chapter Seven: Apostolic Champion

Paul's journey to Jerusalem leads him to Rome, and Robertson associates this with Jesus' last visit to Jerusalem before the crucifixion. In the midst of seeming chaos, there are two things that kept Paul going—his single-minded focus on the mission God had given him and the intervention of the Holy Spirit. Several times along the way, God miraculously intervened in events that could easily have led to his death.

Read Acts 21:1—28:30

Robertson concludes the study of Acts of the Apostles with an echo of the passion of Jesus; this time with Paul on trial for his faith in the resurrection of the dead. But Paul is not finished yet.

■ What is the difference between "Rabbi Saul" and "Paul of Tarsus, Roman citizen"? How has Paul used both of these persons to continue his mission for the gospel?

■ By the time Paul is ready to journey to Rome, how has his understanding of his ministry changed? Robertson explores three tellings of his conversion. What do you discover about Paul by reading each one?

■ What has happened for these changes to occur in Paul?

■ What are the charges that Paul specifically faces in Jerusalem?

■ What parallels do you see with Paul's "trial and defense" and that of Jesus?

■ How do Paul's continuous appeals to high authorities continue to promote the gospel? Or do they hurt his cause?

What have been the featured elements of Paul's prophetic ministry?

■ Healing
■ Preaching
■ Teaching
■ Others?

Luke invites the reader to faith in Jesus Christ despite the visible hardships that we have read throughout Acts.

- How would Luke's original audience have reacted to these stories?
- How can we make this message fresh to audiences today?

At the end of Acts, it seems that the result of Paul's ministry was inconclusive. We are left to wonder what happened next.

- If you had been Luke, would you have concluded Acts differently? If so, how?
- What mission has God given you?
- What would it mean for you to boldly trust him in a situation?
- What can you do to strengthen and encourage the Christians around you?
- How would you describe your mission for the rest of your life? What will it take for you to finish well?

Concluding Thoughts

- What are the most significant insights you have gleaned from reading Acts of the Apostles?
- How different are you for having engaged in this study?
- How do you claim the unique apostolic message for yourself and are able to live into the kingdom of God anew?
- Which of Roberton's "apostolic periods" challenges you the most?
  - Call
  - Concord
  - Challenge
  - Change
  - Compromise
  - Colleagues
  - Champion

Sharon Ely Pearson follows her call as a lay minister with a passion for Christian formation. With a home base in Norwalk, Connecticut, her call takes her from coast to coast, equipping others to teach and preach the gospel to children, youth, and adults in a world that is very much like the early church.

SUGGESTIONS
FOR FURTHER READING

Among the best **commentaries** on Acts are James D. G. Dunn, *The Acts of the Apostles*, Epworth Commentaries (London: Epworth, 1997); Joseph A. Fitzmeyer, S.J., *The Acts of the Apostles*, Anchor Bible Series (New York: Doubleday, 1998), Luke Timothy Johnson, *The Acts of the Apostles*, Sacra Pagina Series 5 (Collegeville, MN: Liturgical Press, 1992); William H. Willimon, *Acts* Interpretation (Louisville, KY: John Knox Press, 1988); and Ben Witherington III, *Acts of the Apostles: A Socio-Political Commentary* (Grand Rapids: Eerdmans, 1997).

For a review of the **first-century world**, see Wayne A. Meeks, *The First Urban Christians*, 2nd ed. (New Haven: Yale University Press, 2003); Everett Ferguson, *Backgrounds of Early Christianity* (Grand Rapids: Eerdmans, 2003); James S. Jeffers *The Greco-Roman World of the New Testament* (Downers Grove, IL: InterVarsity, 1999); Robert Louis Wilken, *The First Christians as the Romans Saw Them* (New Haven: Yale University Press, 2003); and Ben Witherington III, *The Indelible Image: The Theological and Ethical World of the New Testament,* The Individual Witnesses, vol. 1 (Downers Grove, IL: InterVarsity, 2009).

For a glimpse into the nature and effects of **Paul's conversion**, see Richard N. Longenecker, *The Road from Damascus: The Impact of Paul's Conversion on His Life, Thought, and Ministry* (Grand Rapids: Eerdmans, 2002); and Richard V. Peace and David M. Scholer, *Conversion in the New Testament: Paul and the Twelve* (Grand Rapids: Eerdmans, 1999).

For more on the **apostolic mission**, see James D. G. Dunn, *Beginning in Jerusalem, Christianity in the Making,* vol. 2 (Grand Rapids: Eerdmans, 2009); and B. J. Oropeza, C. K. Robertson, and Douglas C. Mohrmann, eds., *Jesus and Paul: Global Perspectives,* Library of New Testament Studies (London: T. & T. Clark, 2010).

ABOUT THE AUTHOR

The Rev. Canon C. K. Robertson, Ph.D. is Canon to the Presiding Bishop of The Episcopal Church, having previously served as Canon to the Ordinary in the Diocese of Arizona and Honorary Canon for the Diocese of Dar Es Salaam in Africa. A Fellow of the Episcopal Church Foundation, Dr. Robertson earned a doctorate in New Testament at Durham University, where he studied with James D. G. Dunn, Lightfoot Professor of Divinity. Currently he is Distinguished Visiting Professor at The General Theological Seminary.

He has also worked extensively with the Department of Education, the White House, and Hollywood studios and guilds as Executive Director of *Film Clips, Inc.* Dr. Robertson serves on several national boards and has published many books and articles, including *Transforming Stewardship* (2009) and, with B. J. Oropeza and Douglas C. Mohrmann, *Jesus and Paul: Global Perspectives* (2010).